TARGET FO

"DAY BY DAY CONTEMPLATE YOUR COUNTRY'S POWER TILL YOU GROW FULL OF PASSIONATE LOVE FOR HER. AND WHEN YOU REALISE HER GREATNESS, REMEMBER THAT IT WAS THE DEAD WHO WON IT FOR YOU."

THUCYDIDES

Wearing anti-gas clothing and gasmasks a section of the AFS carry out an exercise in the forecourt of the Dover Road Fire Station in 1939.

Several private cars were requisitioned by local government under the War Emergency Act. In this photograph can be seen a modified private car used by the AFS to tow a trailer pump and carry a ladder.

TARGET FOLKESTONE

Roy Humphreys

MERESBOROUGH BOOKS
1990

Published by Meresborough Books, 17 Station Road, Rainham, Kent. ME8 7RS.

Meresborough Books is a specialist publisher of books about Kent. A list of titles currently available will be found at the back of this book. They include 'A Pictorial Study of Hawkinge Parish' and 'A Pictorial Study of Alkham Parish', both by Roy Humphreys, the latter with Susan Lees. Another book by Roy Humphreys 'Hawkinge 1912-1961', a history of the former RAF Station, is planned to be reprinted in 1991, together with 'Kent Airfields in the Battle of Britain' to which he is a contributor.

ISBN 0948193 514

Printed by Biddles Ltd, Guildford.

CONTENTS

ACKNOWLEDGEMENTS

An Englishman's patriotism is often presented in peace-time as a mere emotional affair, and yet in time of war, nothing can be further from the truth. His instincts prompt him to be a free man and so it is not so surprising amidst the harshness and uncertainty of war that he finds comradeship and pride of achievement.

Being a powerful emotion in most people, nostalgia has induced a willingness and generosity in some Folkestonians, and indeed others, whose contributions to this work are acknowledged with gratitude.

I am, therefore, indebted to the following: Wing Commander C. Beaston (Retired); Ken Owen, Secretary KAHRS; Winston G. Ramsey, Editor of 'After The Battle'; Alan F. Taylor, Secretary of the Folkestone and District Local History Society; John Guy, Secretary of the Kent Defence Research Group; David Collyer, Archivist to the Kent Aviation Historical Research Society; Eric Hart; Sidney Lester; Alfred Gray; Richard Crane; Jerome Jahnke (USA); Colin Parker; Percy Bricknell; David Radford; Len Snook; William "Scotty" Lester; Bert Blackford; Ted Newman; William G.M. Watson; John Mellor; the staff of the Guildhall Camera Centre, particularly Ken Hall; and staff of the Folkestone Reference Library; L.H. Gurney; T. White; Brian Hart; Jim Meaker; P. May; Ken Stace Paine; Dr Ian Lindsay; Ian Gagan; John Glover; 'Kent Messenger'; 'Folkestone Herald'; Edith Winton; Eileen Hall; Kathleen Nash; E. Rees; Daphne Pegel; Jean Mee; B.M. Vant; Beatty Macdonald; Margaret Simons; Gladys Hazzard; Joan Sharpe; Lily May; Mrs Atkins; Mrs V.A. Fenton; Daisy Evans.

INTRODUCTION

There is little doubt that my attempt to tell the story of Folkestone's war years was begun at least twenty years too late.

The subject is bigger than I at first anticipated, and in the end I am scarcely scratching the surface of it. Much of the admiration the outsider might feel about Folkestone and its citizens, after the narrative unfolds to its conclusion, must inevitably derive from the existing records, newspaper reports and the survivors.

The documents upon which this book is based, without which I hasten to add, I should have been quite helpless, are the "Borough of Folkestone Resumé of Enemy Action — September 3rd 1939, Onwards", the incomplete "Borough of Folkestone Air Raid Precautions Department Operational Reports", and a list of incidents originally held by the Chief Warden, Lt Colonel C.A. Clark, DSO, MC.

Through the narrative, photographs, maps and selected memorabilia, this book will, despite some gaps and many variations in the recorded data, reveal how the town and its citizens endured the traumas of war.

It is to the citizens of Folkestone, who willingly gave their services to the town, that this book is dedicated.

Company Commanders of the 8th (Cinque Ports) Battalion, Home Guard, were inspected by Lt General Sir Edmund Schreiber, KCB, DSO, C-in-C, South Eastern Command. Also present are Brigadier O.P. Edgecumbe, CBE, MC, Lt Colonel W.H. Gribben, CMG, CBE (Battalion Commander), and his Adjutant, Captain C. Foreman.   (via Brian Hart)

THE PRELUDE TO WAR

Soon after the Air Raid Precautions Act was passed in 1937, the Chief Constable of Folkestone, A.S. Beesley, was seeking responsible citizens to form the nucleus of an ARP system in the town. After acceptance applicants were enrolled in a register and were given a number to avoid any confusion with people of similar surnames.

The Chief Constable was in sole charge of the organisation until the appointment of Lt Colonel A. Murray-Smith, OBE, as Chief Air Raid Warden. In September 1938 Murray-Smith resigned and was succeeded by H.C. Green, who remained in that post until February 1940, when Lt Colonel C.A. Clark, DSO, MC, took over and served in that capacity throughout the rest of the war.

In July 1938 it was the responsibility of the ARP to fit respirators to every permanent resident in the borough who were to attend at one of the four fitting stations — Chichester Hall, Sandgate, The Old Council Offices, Cheriton, the Town Hall, Folkestone, and the Salvation Army HQ in Bradstone Road.

In October that same year every household was visited to check that everyone was in possession of a respirator and, at the same time, wardens had been instructed to make their first census. Wardens continued to make regular census lists of residents within the borough throughout the war period.

It was not generally known that census details were used by the authorities to filter-out and discriminate against persons who were not bona fide residents and who may have had more sinister, or obscure, reasons for occupying a household.

If any air raid warden had any doubts about the importance of his or her job then they were soon dispelled by the pamphlet issued to all of them by their new chief — Colonel Clark. His attitude and enthusiasm was totally military and his little pamphlet left no one in any doubt that the ARP system in Folkestone was going to be run on firm discipline.

The opening lines of "A Call to Duty" ran thus: "I want to impress on all wardens the vital importance of their duties. An army in the field is responsible for its own protection, and this is provided for in the form of 'out-posts'. You wardens are the outposts of the Home Front, and are, therefore, responsible for the protection of your fellow citizens. On your vigilance, courage and promptitude depend the lives of your fellow men."

He finished his composition: "Let us then be up and doing, gird yourselves with enthusiasm for your great work, be continuously on the alert, show the spirit and magnanimity of our great people. Infuse courage, love of duty, and

"S.M. Cleeve", the 9.2-inch gun of the 4th Super-Heavy Battery, RA, on a railway siding at Hythe Station in October 1940.   (I.W.M.)

the will and spirit to overcome the bestial tyranny that the enemy would impose upon the free peoples of the world.

"Cheerfulness, watchfulness, efficiency and devotion to duty must be our watchword."

Above all, Colonel Clark had that British eccentricity of purpose — unshakable, resolute and an ability to get the best out of his subordinates. During the intensive period of enemy shelling there were many occasions when the military discipline imposed by Colonel Clark was underlined by the sheer courage of his flock.

I can mention only one occasion here, but there were many others. Observation posts, without any formal cover in the shell-swept areas of the town, were manned at night by a few ARP personnel who had already done a day's work. Colonel Clark recalled one such night when he happened to visit the Stade Post at 1.00 am.

"The light was in the post but no one was inside. I went outside and was walking towards the devastated Beech Street area when I stumbled into a solitary warden — a woman. It was very dark and I felt an uncanniness in the air. She told me one warden had gone to Dover Street and another towards the Royal Pavilion Hotel area. Each had gone out on a lone search whilst shells were falling all around them."

Colonel Clark had often thought of that woman and every time he did so it deepened his admiration of human nature. "I am . . ." he had said, ". . . very proud to have served with them for so long, and I will always think of the wardens with gratitude and affection."

"The Cheriton Group had not had its fair share of glamour . . ." so read one report, ". . . but part of their duties had been bomb reconnaissance in the rural areas. Out of some ninety unexploded ack-ack shells, the Cheriton Group had been responsible for dealing with over sixty."

The prominent part played by the ARP services in Folkestone has faded in memory, like the brown pages of the official documents and old newspapers, since their Stand Down on 1st June 1945. Collectively known as the Civil Defence Services, men and women of the rescue teams and first aid teams worked together in whatever circumstances prevailed. The war had, through the constant traumas of enemy action of one sort or another, thrown these dedicated men and women together in one cause. They were united into one workable unit that was rated second to none.

In July 1945, a fitting tribute was paid to Chief Inspector R.J. Butcher, ARP Sub-Controller, at an informal ceremony held in the Town Hall. He was given a beautifully inscribed album in which was written:

"To Chief Inspector Butcher, BEM, Civil Defence Sub-Controller, Folkestone area, this address is subscribed by members of the Civil Defence organisations of Folkestone and Corporation staff, with whom you have worked in close collaboration.

"We wish to place on record an appreciation of the splendid services you have rendered to the CD organisation of the borough throughout the period of the Second World War.

"Your force of example and masterful handling of serious incidents caused by enemy action were highly commendable; your power of organisation and administration were of the highest order; and your untiring energy and boundless activity were a source of inspiration to all."

There has never been any doubt that the town can lay claim to the emotive title "Front-Line Folkestone", just as its neighbour can lay claim to "Front-Line Dover". Of course, the whole county of Kent was in the "Front-Line" during 1939 to 1945, and the South East in particular became known the world over as "Hell-Fire Corner".

Royal Marine ratings of "A" Battery, 1st Heavy Anti-Aircraft Regiment of the Marine Naval Base Defence Organisation (MNBDO), were deployed at Hope Farm, Crete Road East, above Folkestone, with four 3-inch guns of World War One vintage. Fresh from their depot at Lymstone, Dorset, they dug gun-pits and dug-outs and lived for many weeks without removing their clothing. During the Battle of Britain it was not unusual for each gun to have fired 118 shells in any one action. "A" Battery were credited with shooting down over thirty-eight enemy aircraft from June to December 1940. Ironically, "A" Battery were posted from Crete Road to the island of Crete in December 1940, where over half their number were either killed or taken prisoner.   (J. Meaker)

Within these pages various aspects of war-torn Folkestone might appear only loosely connected with the main theme. I make no apology for their inclusion because they add the "feel" of everyday life at the time. The temptation to record in detail political and military strategy has been resisted for the very reason that war with its strategic implications of bombing and shelling meant little to the ordinary citizen. He, like the combatants who fought in aerial battles over the town, was just a pawn in a game. Although oblivious of the influences of such military strategy he was acutely aware of the senseless destruction of his home town and the horrific loss of life.

And yet, as the war unfolded, it became poignantly clear, as buildings they had known since birth collapsed under heavy bombardment, that the citizens of Folkestone developed, almost overnight, a camaraderie of spirit which was so typical of the British, a spirit which almost always is misunderstood by her enemies.

Dr Robert Lindsay, GM, MA, MB, ChB, who lived at Copula House, Dover Road, Folkestone, was the town's second George Medallist. A Scot by birth, he moved to Folkestone from Manchester in 1936, setting up his practice in the Dover Road area, where he became a family GP to many residents who remember him to this day with affection and respect. Dr Lindsay was not a well man. He died on 4th November 1943, at the age of fifty-three.

(Dr Ian Lindsay)

George Fenton, a carpenter of Dolphins Road, Folkestone, was awarded the George Medal for his part in rescuing an injured man who had been blown up by land-mines at the Royal Pavilion Hotel, in October 1942.   (Mrs V.A. Fenton)

In 1939 the town was still wrapped in its Edwardian milieu, a seaside town which could boast of its quaint streets and lanes together with a harbour where images of smuggling activities were conjured from the old buildings. Spreading to the west of the town were the many hotels and boarding houses which stood above the curious zig-zag paths winding around the face of the cliff between seashore and The Leas.

People have looked across the English Channel for hundreds of years and on a clear day observed the cliffs of France. But in June 1940, they looked across that narrow strip of water to see, in their mind's eye, a powerful enemy poised to strike. Folkestone eventually was to endure almost every form of modern aerial attack, ranging from high explosive bombs, parachute mines, incendiary devices, large calibre shells, fighter-bomber attacks and the flying bomb.

The town was battered because it happened to be an area above which enemy bomber formations flew to and from other targets; because it happened to be within range of the German long-range coastal guns situated in the Calais – Boulogne sector; because it also was in easy reach of the Messerschmitt and Focke-Wulf fighter-bombers on their Seerauberangriff attacks.

Because row upon row of terraced houses were either demolished or badly damaged in the fighter-bomber raids, it was generally believed by the public, whose opinions were often provoked by press statements, that such callousness was in violation of the Geneva Convention. And yet those Luftwaffe fighter-bomber pilots possessed a calibre of bravado and expertise which could only be matched by our own fighter aces. There is no doubt that a mutual respect existed between them. The German pilots were briefed to attack a particular target, either gas-holders, electricity stations, railways or gun emplacements.

In the absurdity of modern warfare mistakes happened. Peace-time absurdity after nearly fifty years is that bomb-sites still exist in the town.

At the outbreak of war the population of Folkestone was 47,800. Voluntary evacuation resulted in over 37,000 persons leaving the borough in 1940. An informal census taken by wardens in 1941 showed the population to be 14,500, and by 1943 this total had reached 19,000, of which no fewer than 3,500 were children.

Opinions vary about the sense of it all but the ranks of the essential services swelled as a result, largely because an additional, and unforeseen, workload suddenly became apparent. And so the Special War Reserves Constabulary, the National Fire Service, fire spotters, Women's Voluntary Service, nurses, ARP rescue teams and the Home Guard progressively benefited.

Police responsibility seemed endless. From 3rd September 1939 there evolved intense activity in preparing and enforcing the black-out restrictions, checking the lighting regulations for motor vehicles and rounding-up aliens. Even the positioning and efficiency of the warning sirens was a police matter. Additionally, they had the influx of foreign nationals to contend with and the constant reminder that "fifth-columnists" might infiltrate our shores. Many fruitless hours were spent investigating reports concerning illicit wireless transmissions, low flying aircraft being signalled from the ground and small boats running up onto beaches at the dead of night.

Historians are not alone in their disagreements with official documents and authoritative statements appearing in published works. Sometimes, after pains-taking research, one can realise that important historical works are occasionally in error on some minor point or other.

And then there are the people who can remember a particular incident and regard their intimate knowledge of the subject, despite the passage of time, to be almost unshakable. But the reading public, and more especially the enthu-siast, may often wonder whether memory can be trusted after nearly fifty years.

Nevertheless, when the war had drawn to a close, hundreds of civilians had been recruited and trained and were skilled members of teams whose count-less, and largely unrewarded, acts of unselfish heroism earned them the highest commendation.

1940

In July 1939, between the hours of darkness from Saturday 8th to Sunday 9th, the town was subjected to its first black-out test. It was the first of many such tests before the black-out regulations became incumbent upon the public, who hitherto had regarded all war-like instruction with scepticism. Nevertheless, the tests were part of the Air Raid Precaution Act introduced in 1937 and mobilised a year later.

Folkestonians had already received dozens of leaflets telling them how to screen their windows with black cloth; how to cover the glass panes with brown sticky-tape and to use their sidelights only on their cars. Now the sirens sounded in the "ALERT" mode at 10 pm. A number of responsible citizens, carrying tin hats and gas masks, rushed to first aid posts, ARP warden posts, equipment storage depots and all types of air raid shelters, above and beneath ground. Special war reserve constables peddled furiously to prearranged places where they phoned-in to a central control. An hour later the "ALL CLEAR" was sounded on the strategically sited sirens.

Probably the first casualty of the war in Folkestone occurred on 17th December 1939, when a 78-year-old man was knocked down and killed by a car while crossing a road at night. "It was," the coroner remarked at the inquest, ". . . another of those black-out fatalities." Incidents of a similar kind were to escalate as the war progressed.

Back in September 1939 the Government had decided to evacuate London on a voluntary basis and, while such a decision was an emotive one and totally praiseworthy, to select Folkestone to receive an estimated 13,000 children was, in hindsight, foolhardy in the extreme. Fortunately only a fraction of that total arrived, due in part to worried parents refusing to send their offspring. Nevertheless, securely labelled and carrying cardboard boxed gas-masks, 1,600 children arrived at Central Station, representing 23 London schools.

Daphne Pegel recalls: "Our lessons in Folkestone were taken in various centres to avoid too great a concentration of girls in any one spot. They were held in two Baptist church halls, two Anglican church halls, a convent and my favourite, the Deep Sea Mission in the harbour. Eventually we gained permission to use Westbourne House, Coolinge Lane, a delightful oak-panelled house vacated by a boys' preparatory school who had sensibly been evacuated elsewhere. I was billeted in Melrose Hotel, Marine Parade, and in private houses in Cheriton Road and Grimston Gardens. The luckier girls were boarded in Westbourne House."

Police Constable Cyril "Taffy" Williams, GM, Folkestone Borough Police Force, joined in 1934, then transferred to the Traffic Division at Sandgate. He served in Folkestone throughout the war years and was awarded the George Medal in 1942, when he rescued an injured man when a minefield exploded at the Royal Pavilion Hotel.   (Mrs K.W. Atkins)

"C" Company 1st Battalion Middlesex Regiment were assembled in the garden of St Mary's Convent, Shorncliffe Road, to have their photograph taken in 1943. They shared facilities with the National Fire Service until the battalion was moved out just after "D" Day.   (P. May)

In a Christmas message, given at their festive party, Councillor Wright told the evacuees that the Folkestone Aldermen and Councillors were very glad to see them safely housed in Folkestone, and were also glad to know they were all happy.

Daphne remembered: "The first winter of the war was bitterly cold and some days we were unable to get to school, as Coolinge Lane was blocked with snow and ice. But I remember the daffodils on the Leas and the lovely rockery flowers down the zig-zag paths. At that time the beaches were clear of defences and anti-invasion devices, and so we were able to wander everywhere, eating ice-creams bought from Rossi's Ice Cream Parlour, Marine Parade, before he was interned."

But Daphne remembered also a tragic accident: "Hearing a strange noise one day and looking out of the bedroom window I saw a Hawkinge aerodrome plane showing a large yellow light at the back suddenly nose-dive in front of Caesars Camp. My friend and I ran towards the crash in time to see the pilot's torso being removed from the burning plane. Neither my friend nor I were upset at the gruesome scene (as I might be now) and we were definitely thrilled at a later date when we found an arm washed up on the beach below the Leas!"

The luckless pilot who had met an untimely death was Sergeant Lomay of 3 Squadron, then based at RAF Hawkinge. By strange coincidence the investigating officer at the scene of the crash was Flt Lt Charles Beaston, Adjutant of 16 Army Co-operation Squadron, also based at Hawkinge, and who had been the next-door neighbour of Daphne at Eltham.

Retired Wing Commander Beaston recalled the argument in the billiards room one evening when the point to be settled was that a Lysander aircraft could get away from a German fighter by a tight turn and its slower speed. The result was a loss of height and a dive to earth for Sgt Lomay.

"I have thought of this crash many times since," Beaston said, ". . . and I am firmly convinced the pilot was an exceedingly brave man who controlled his crashing plane away from the school, houses and hospital to a spot in the centre of an open space."

Wednesday 3rd January. *The Chief Constable of Kent reported that four mines were washed ashore at Dungeness this morning. These have been rendered harmless.*

Despite mines being washed up on the beaches from Dungeness to Seabrook, the spirit of patriotism was yet to be fired in Folkestonians, although they had been receiving all kinds of leaflets through their letter boxes warning them and instructing them on, "What to do if . . ."

Since 1936 there had been a steady trickle of refugees fleeing Europe through the port of Folkestone, but on 3rd January quite a different sort of refugee arrived causing some excitement. After being in Germany since before the outbreak of war, Miss Unity Freeman-Mitford, the 25-year-old daughter of Lord

During the Battle of Britain, a Spitfire Fund was arranged to enable the public to purchase an aircraft of that type and which would carry the name of the town, city, industrial manufacturer, British Colonies and certain wealthy individuals. In Folkestone, as in other towns, donations were made in a variety of ways and a cheque for £5,000, dated 5th February 1941, was sent to Lord Beaverbrook by the 'Folkestone & Hythe District Herald'. Above: the Spitfire Mk IIb P8467, which carried the name Folkestone & Hythe, was a Presentation Spitfire serving with No. 131 Squadron RAF.   (Imperial War Museum)

and Lady Redesdale, accompanied by her mother and sister Deborah, arrived in England by ferry from Boulogne. The return to England by Miss Mitford created considerable public interest for several reasons, one being a report that early in September 1939, at Munich, she had been shot and wounded in the head. It was also reported that Hitler had personally provided a special train to take Miss Mitford, a close friend of the German leader, from Munich to Switzerland for the journey home.

Unity's arrival at Folkestone Harbour was said to be as good as a pantomime and provided excellent comedy. Over half of Fleet Street had arrived to meet her, but for some reason the authorities decided that they should not see her. Soldiers with fixed bayonets were on duty at the harbour entrance and a large contingent of police were instructed to keep everyone away from the harbour.

But despite the precautions Unity's landing was observed by many people, including the more astute Fleet Street journalists. One of them wrote afterwards: "She has no appearance of hardened confidence about her. She is, in fact, very pretty and, if I may say so, rather gives the impression of a nervous, retiring disposition. She was not wearing a Swastika when she arrived at the

Numerous First Aid Teams shared facilities with ARP posts. "C" Group (Cheriton), although initially based at Baker Road, also manned the Cheriton Road sports ground. Above: this FAP team was photographed in 1944 at the sports ground.   (Lilian May)

harbour and she had no apparent injury. She was able to walk, somewhat haltingly, but she certainly looked pale and ill."

Lord Redesdale had stayed overnight at the Royal Pavilion Hotel, close to the harbour, to await his daughter's arrival and to take her to the family home at High Wycombe.

Unity was the sister-in-law of the British Fascist leader, Oswald Mosley, and had spent many weekends with Hitler at his Berchtesgaden home. Hitler's mistress, Eva Braun, had once called Unity "that English Valkyrie". Miss Mitford had been fascinated by the German leader and, when hostilities began between the two countries, she had shot herself in the head. Unity Mitford died of meningitis in 1948.

Thursday 4th January. *Kent County Police reported that at 0020 hrs today a mine was washed ashore 100 yards from the Lade look-out near Lydd.*

Like most other seaside towns in Kent, whose source of income largely depended on summer tourism, Folkestone became a sensitive area. Tourism began to decline when war started. A few enemy aircraft were plotted around the Kent coast which caused the sirens to wail their mournful note of warning.

Pamphlets galore dropped through letter boxes — "What to do If . . ." Few people read them. They were used to light fires and pipes, although the more discerning put them away in living room sideboards for safe keeping — just in case!

The "ALL CLEAR" sounded many hours later which annoyed the local shop-keepers rather more than the ordinary civilian who viewed the whole procedure quite unperturbed.

One or two anti-aircraft guns had fired a salvo at what appeared to be dubious targets. All sorts of rumours circulated in the town when a Folkestone fishing trawler, FE61 — *Young Harry*, was lost with all hands. It had, almost certainly, struck a mine. British, German and even French mines slipped their cables in heavy seas and were a constant menace to shipping in the Channel.

Sunday 7th January. *Two British mines have been washed ashore near Hythe.*
Hitler's armies were soon to overwhelm the French forces and engage the British Expeditionary Force in one victory after another, and in rapid succession.

Thursday 11th January. *A British mine was washed ashore near Greatstone.*
Heavy snow falls had blocked most roads leading to the town.

Sunday 14th January. *Sea mines washed ashore at Dungeness.*
The news from the Continent was particularly grim and the weather this side of the English Channel was miserable in the extreme.

The role of the Railway Police, during the phase that has become known as "The Phoney War", was no less real to them than the intense activity experienced by the Borough Police Force. The mere suggestion that "fifth-columnists" might infiltrate our shores through the influx of refugees put the Railway Police on their mettle. Above: the Folke-stone Harbour barricade, seen here in July 1940, was manned by Railway Police, who later that same year were assisted by armed sentries.   (I.W.M.)

Sunday 21st January. *Heavy snow falls.*

"Mein Kampf" — in an 18-part weekly series costing sixpence (2½p) per copy. The first issue dealt with Hitler's youth, his years of study and suffering in Vienna. The royalties from the sales went to the British Red Cross Society!

Monday 29th January. *Mines washed ashore at Folkestone, Hythe and Dymchurch.*

Since early January German mine-laying aircraft had been observed over the English Channel during the night. The weather was particularly foul at this time with heavy snow falls and early morning frosts. Sergeant Body from New Romney, who had joined the Territorial Army long before there was any hint of hostilities with Germany, moved his searchlight and associated equipment of the 386th Searchlight Battery to a bleak site near Abbotts Cliff, Capel le Ferne. The site he chose was in a very exposed position. The crew had been given an old motor coach — seats removed, in which to live. Another searchlight was sited near the railway line in the Warren. Perhaps the only redeeming feature to offset the detachments' miserable existence was the daily rum ration of one bottle between ten men.

How long this disguised pillbox, "Jai de la Joie", erected near the Leas Cliff Hall in 1940, would have fooled German invading troops is anyone's guess.   (I.W.M.)

Another disguised pillbox. Police Constable Crane recalled: ". . . my attention was drawn to a man in French Naval uniform who was taking pictures of the harbour area. He proved to be on leave from the French Navy Ministry in Paris and was accompanied by an English woman who was said to be the wife of another French Naval Officer. I was told the photographs were of Folkestone fishermen, but as the officer did not have a permit to take pictures of this kind I seized the film. The officer caught the 12.15 pm boat to France and the lady, who came from the west country, stated she would be back in Folkestone within three weeks to collect the film."   (I.W.M.)

Tuesday 30th January. *Folkestone control reports that a mine exploded in contact with the mattress of the East Cliff Defence Works.*

Heavy seas soon displaced mines from their cradles and during the night one of them exploded against the rocks at the base of the East Cliff. The blast blew out windows in 46 houses within a radius of 600 yards at cliff level. The estimated damage was from £2,000 to £4,000. In two houses the ceilings had fallen upon unsuspecting sleeping occupants. The only injury was to a young girl who received a cut eye when the family was thrown from their beds. When her parents picked themselves up from the floor her mother was heard to say: ". . . Hitler's here at last!"

Thursday 8th February. *Mine washed ashore at Dungeness.*

The British people were left with few illusions about what to expect if war with Germany got out of hand. Through the medium of the national newspapers and various magazines there often appeared articles by H.G. Wells and others, who warned about large scale air attacks. Even the Imperial Defence Committee had estimated that air attacks launched upon the capital city would probably last just sixty days, with a casualty list numbering 600,000 killed and twice as many injured.

However, by mid-February, few people in Folkestone bothered to carry their gas-masks any more and family air raid shelters were still stacked-up and rusting, unassembled in council yards.

But despite this measure of complacency work had, albeit tentatively, begun on coastal defences, and a large number of halls were reserved in the town to house homeless families should the need ever arise. Every week someone, somewhere in the town, was summoned to appear at the magistrates court for black-out offences. Fines were usually kept to a minimum by kindly magistrates who understood the difficulties of the elderly and the zeal of the ARP wardens and policemen.

Appearing at the Leas Cliff Hall was Sir Malcolm Campbell who gave a series of lectures called "The Romance of the Blue Bird", which outlined his world-wide adventures with his famous, record breaking racing car.

On the other side of the coin a 20 year old mechanic was arrested on suspicion of being a German spy. Of German descent he was found to have maps of Folkestone in his possession, but he denied being a spy and said he could only speak broken German as he was educated in England. He was acquitted and given a warning.

Friday 22nd March (Good Friday)

During the "phoney war" period the Luftwaffe was yet to demonstrate its powers over the civilian population and the only excitement in the town was usually provided by the ARP exercises.

While additional accommodation was still being sought in Hythe for more evacuees expected to arrive from Gravesend, the streets, roads and lanes of

Set in a tidy garden opposite Dr Barnardos Home, in Wear Bay Crescent, was the concrete Warden's Post of the "H" Group Harbour ARP. Seated from left to right are: Group Head Warden, D. "Mac" McSwan; Lt Colonel C.A. Clarke, DSO, MC, Chief Air Raid Warden; Mrs Lillian Allen; Mrs Annie Williams; Chief Inspector R.J. Butcher, ARP Sub-Controller. On either side of Mr Teacher, who holds the post's mascot, "Tiddly-Winks", are the two Radford brothers, David and John, who became known as "the live-wire messengers". Standing extreme right is R.W. "Jack" Hogben.

Folkestone were littered with all sorts of "staged" incidents. Tied to stretchers, suitably bandaged "volunteers" were being lowered out of bedroom windows in one street, while in another, stirrup-pumps were being aimed at little pots of burning tar simulating incendiary bombs.

The Special War Reserve Constables, carrying their military-style gas-masks, were out in force manning dozens of temporary road barriers, whilst control room staff were trying to make some sense out of hundreds of messages, either received by telephone or handed-in by fifteen-year-old boys on bicycles.

Somehow the seriousness of these exercises was mis-placed in the minds of the ordinary citizen. Perhaps this was because the average tin-hatted ARP warden, who most often was the man next door, unlike the special constable or the AFS member, became a father figure in the community.

Sunday 24th March. *Richard Tauber, one of the finest concert tenors of his day, sang at the Leas Cliff Hall.*

Tauber was of German descent but when he visited Folkestone it was as an Englishman, for only three days before his concert he had received his natural-isation papers. There seemed little doubt that part of the generous applause he received was almost certainly attributable to that fact.

Sunday 31st March. *Air raid siren test at 9.30 am.*

There was a surprisingly large number of visitors still in the town. They seemed to have extended their Easter holiday and may have felt it was the last opportunity to visit Folkestone. At the Central Cinema Joan Crawford and Norma Shearer were in "The Woman"; at the Playhouse Cinema there was "The Saint in London", starring George Sanders; and at the Savoy Cinema, Deanna Durbin starred in "First Love".

Wednesday 10th April. *Their Majesties the King and Queen visited East Kent. The King inspected troops at Shorncliffe Barracks while the Queen went to inspect the London Scottish HQ at Broome Park.*

Friday 10th May. *Hitler launched his attacks on Belgium and Holland. Winston Churchill became Prime Minister.*

Saturday 11th May. *Kent police move to arrest aliens.*

At 8 am police moved to arrest several hundred aliens. Of the 175 detained, 21 came from Folkestone, including a doctor who had a practice in the town. Both civil and military police called at homes of all male enemy aliens, and by 10 pm that day those arrested were taken under escort to internment camps. Other aliens were required to report daily to the police station and were told they must not use any form of transport and were under a personal curfew between the hours of 8 pm and 6 am. Anyone found without his National Registration Identity Card would be detained for questioning.

In the "Folkestone Herald" for Saturday 11th May, there appeared this notice:

Air Raid Precautions Borough of Folkestone
The emergency committee of the Town Council
strongly advises all members of the public to carry
gas-masks on all occasions.

Signed: Geo. A. Gurr
Mayor

Tuesday 14th May. *Radio appeal by Secretary of State for War.*

The new Secretary of State for War, Anthony Eden, broadcast a message on BBC radio for men to come forward and join a new force of Local Defence Volunteers. It was the beginning of a Home Defence force which was to total many thousands of men from the ages of 18 to 70. It also produced a remarkable effect upon the population who acted on impulse and joined queues outside the police stations to sign-on. At Folkestone, they were still queuing when the Town Hall clock struck midnight. Initally dubbed "parashooters" in local newspapers, the LDV force, under the command of Lt Col K. Kennedy Crauford-Stuart, with his Headquarters at 72 Sandgate Road, were to upset many local people. Doctors, for example, who late at night were attending the sick, were

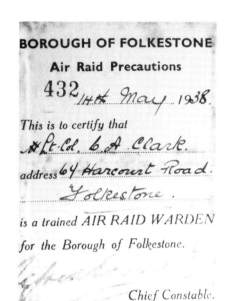

BOROUGH OF FOLKESTONE

Air Raid Precautions

432 /4th May 1938.

This is to certify that

Lt-Col. C.A. Clark.

address 64 Harcourt Road.

Folkestone.

is a trained AIR RAID WARDEN

for the Borough of Folkestone.

Chief Constable.

Signed by Chief Constable Alfred S. Beesley, this ARP membership card was sent to Lt Colonel C.A. Clark, who became the Chief Air Raid Warden of Folkestone.

When Folkestone's Chief Air Raid Warden, Colonel Clark, issued his little pamphlet "A Call to Duty" to all ARP members it instilled in the minds of those who had served in the First World War a sense of comradeship and a style typically of a military genre. Above: members of "C" Group ARP Warden's Post, Baker Road, Cheriton, were encouraged to wear their medal ribbons. One of them wore stripes!

26

constantly challenged and subjected to roadside interrogations. While their identity card was being checked their motorcar was searched. There was at the time an outbreak of spy mania.

Thursday 16th May. *Another warning to general public.*
Local government issued another warning through the medium of the local newspaper: **"Halt who goes there?"**.
It went on to explain that in various localities sentries were posted to guard vulnerable points such as the waterworks, gasworks and electricity stations. These sentries had orders to challenge all persons approaching their post and to fire if the challenge was not replied to.
A courting couple was suddenly challenged by a sentry and the young swain impudently called out "Foe!" Within seconds they found themselves surrounded by over a dozen LDV men, all brandishing pick-axe handles. They spent the night being interrogated by an over-zealous lieutenant.

Friday 17th May. *Swiss subject fined.*
The first offence under the new order forbidding all male aliens to use a motor vehicle was heard at the Folkestone Magistrates Court. A Swiss subject was fined £1 for using a motorcar in the town, after being spotted by PC Page, who had followed the alien to a house in Winifred Road.

Saturday 18th May. *Woman arrested in town.*
An Austrian woman was arrested whilst attending an evening dance at the Leas Cliff Hall. She was in the company of a soldier who was stationed at Shorncliffe Barracks. He became suspicious of her obvious foreign accent and slipped out of the hall to notify the police. She was arrested immediately. It was not so surprising as the national newspapers were reporting that thousands of German parachutists had been dropped behind the Allied Armies in the Low Countries. Arising from these reports was the increased discussions about "fifth-column" saboteurs infiltrating the seaside towns.

Monday 20th May. *Lights burning in windows.*
The population of Folkestone and the surrounding districts were still rather complacent about the black-out regulations. Every week there were reports of lights burning in windows. When PC Duke on 20th saw a light showing from a top window of a house at 10.50 pm, he quite naturally knocked on the door. But he was not prepared for what followed. A man put his head out of a window and said: "What's the matter with you?" When PC Duke informed him of the light the man replied: "You can go to Hell — you must want something better to do on a bright, moonlight night like this!" Appearing in the magistrates court a week later the man was fined £10 or, in default, one month's imprisonment.
Anderson Shelters were, at last, being issued to the general public, but only to those who met with the following conditions outlined in a special notice to all householders.

The Copt Point Battery, East Cliff, Folkestone, was photographed from the air on 22nd July 1940 and shows clearly the two 6-inch naval gun installations on the edge of the cliff. The dense tree area seen left of centre in the picture is the Sanatorium, which had the privilege of being bombed in the first air raid on the town.

"Members of the town who wish to obtain one are asked to communicate as soon as possible with the Acting Borough Engineer at the Council Offices, Church Street. The shelters will be available to the following:
(1) Those who are compulsorily insurable under the National Health Insurance Acts;
(2) People with an income of under £250 a year, or £300 if they have 3 children or more of school age."

Saturday 25th May. *London evacuees lodged in Folkestone since September 1939, left the town en route to Wales.*

It was in this month that Folkestone was to receive its "Big Guns". One of the first installations was at Copt Point, above it would be more correct, but it was always known as the Copt Point Battery locally, although its official name was the Folkestone East Battery. The two 6-inch naval guns had originally served on HMS *Chatham* and HMS *Dublin* in the First World War. The Royal Marine Siege Regiment was responsible for setting-up the battery while civilians under Royal Engineer supervision erected the concrete structures on the East Cliff putting green.

The battery was manned from July 1940 until January 1943, by personnel of 338 Coast Battery, Royal Artillery, but from 1943 onwards there was an interchange of batteries within the 12 Corps area.

The guns were responsible for the defence of the South Coast of England, in particular the eastern side of Folkestone. Their primary role was to engage and sink enemy ships before they could be beached and land troops in the event of an invasion.

Originally the old Coastguard lookout post was used as an observation post but, in April 1943, a new BOP was constructed out of concrete. Also in that year additional weaponry was provided. A 6 pounder anti-tank gun, 4 Spigot mortars and probably the most valuable items to arrive in June were 2 40mm Bofors light anti-aircraft guns, housed in special concrete emplacements.

To begin with personnel were accommodated in the East Cliff Pavilion, but when numbers increased, billets were provided in nearby private houses. For example, 29 Wear Bay Road became the Battery Office; 30 became the Officers' Mess while 32, 33 and 34 were requisitioned for other ranks. In February 1941 3 Varne Road became the Sergeants' Mess and the Pavilion was used as a NAAFI, incorporating a cook-house, dining hall and recreation facilities. On either side of the battery position there were installed searchlights supplied by a 22KV Lister Generating Set.

Another twin-gun installation was situated above the harbour on ground which originally had been used for recreation, adjacent to the St Andrew's Convalescent Home, with East Cliff Gardens on one side and Wear Bay Road on the other. Officially known as Folkestone West Battery, it too had a pair of 6-inch naval guns used in the First World War, and was handed over to 339 Heavy Battery, RA, in July 1940. Classed as an "Emergency Battery" its role was purely anti-invasion and its effectiveness was limited, neither gun could depress to a range below 800 yards and an area of "dead-water" existed on the far side of the harbour for a distance of 1,800 yards! The Battery Observation Post for this installation was situated in 12 Wear Bay Road, while the billets for personnel were in private houses and in "Tatts"'s Boarding House, East Cliff.

Two more searchlights were installed. No.1 was housed in a single building of brick and concrete near the Victoria Pier, while the other was placed halfway down the cliff face to the east of the guns. Their effective range in good visibility was about 6,000 yards.

On 26th May 1942 339 Coast Battery was replaced by 413 Coast Battery, but in September that year the establishment was reduced. This reduction in manning levels was made up by No.5 Platoon "B" Company, 8th (Cinque Ports) Battalion, Home Guard.

Folkestone West Battery received two Spigot Mortars and one 40mm Bofors in May 1943, the latter making its debut on the 25th and going into action against FW190s on a "Tip-and-run" raid.

On 23rd December 1943 a German long-range shell partly demolished Nos 3 and 4 Wear Bay Road which resulted in a permanent evacuation of those billets.

The third gun emplacement was known as Mill Point Battery. By far the largest, it comprised four 5.5-inch naval guns, originally part of the armaments of HMS *Hood*, situated on the Leas directly in front of Clifton Crescent. The role

Folkestone West Battery's installation of two 6-inch naval guns is easily identified in this aerial photograph taken on 6th October 1940. Other features are also instantly recognisable, such as St Andrew's Convalescent Home, the railway viaduct, the gasworks and Beach Street, which was flattened in November 1940 by a parachute mine.

of this battery was similar to the other two on the East Cliff, although their responsibility was directed against enemy attacks on the harbour and the western approaches to the beaches in the event of an invasion. Personnel of 412 Coastal Battery manned the guns and were billeted in Clifton Crescent. The Battery Observation Post was specially built on the edge of the Leas, almost in line with Earls Avenue. This battery was reduced to "Care and Maintenance" in November 1943.

The Capel Battery, although not directly under the control of Folkestone Fire Command, is mentioned here because of its closeness to the town. It was late in preparation and construction and did not report "ready for action" until 26th June 1942, making its first engagement on 24th August that year when it fired two shells.

The object of this battery was to engage enemy shipping passing through the English Channel, to protect Allied convoys from surface attacks, and to make "counter bombardment" against enemy shipping supporting an invasion. It was further required to engage enemy minelaying activities and to act in support of air defence of both Dover and Folkestone Harbours.

The three 8-inch guns were electrically operated, could be elevated to 70 degrees for ack-ack purposes and had a range estimated at 31,000 yards. To combat low-flying enemy aircraft the battery received two 40mm Bofors guns in

May 1943, which let fly at every aircraft in the vicinity, friend or foe. The last heavy shell fired by the 8-inch guns was on 31st October 1943. The total rounds fired came to 30, seven of which were fired in the ack-ack mode.

The first ack-ack guns deployed near and around Folkestone belonged to "A" Battery 1st Heavy Anti-aircraft Regiment, Royal Marines, who had arrived from their depot at Lympstone, Devon, in April 1940. After only eight weeks' training the Marines dug pits to accommodate their 3-inch guns, formerly the armament of a First World War destroyer; on land above Hope Farm, Crete Road East. Their only living quarters were dug-outs and trenches, sandbagged and roofed with corrugated sheets of galvanised iron. "A" Battery took up positions at Hope Farm (D11), Ridge Row (D12), Coolinge Lane (D14) and at Upper Arpinge Farm (D16). The Hope Farm gunners were credited with shooting down thirty-eight enemy aircraft before they were posted abroad in December 1940. Ironically they found themselves defending the island of Crete, where over half their numbers were either killed or taken prisoner of war when Crete was overrun by superior German Forces.

Sunday 26th May. *Over 9,000 refugees land at Folkestone.*

Spy mania was becoming a headache for both police and immigration authorities. Since September 1939, all civilian cross-channel traffic had been diverted from the port of Dover to Folkestone. This also included the Belgian Marine's Ostend boats, as no other vessel was allowed to enter Dover without special Admiralty permission.

There were many peculiar incidents and most will never be told, but Police Constable Richard Crane was given a task which he recalled in his memoirs: "Not One of the Heavy Mob":

"During the days preceding Dunkirk, ships and boats of all kinds were anchored off Folkestone awaiting their turn to enter harbour to discharge refugees, soldiers, prisoners of war and others fleeing from the Germans. The refugees were interrogated closely as it was not expected the Germans would forego such an opportunity to infiltrate spies. The German prisoners of war were taken in batches to London with police as escort. It was during the time of this abnormal activity at Folkestone harbour when I was on reserve duty one evening. I was singled out by the Chief Inspector who was accompanied by an English-speaking Frenchman. This man had come across the English Channel with a large French lorry with its tarpaulin cover securely fastened down. My job was to find a safe refuge for the vehicle for the night and to watch over it until relieved in the morning. I was supplied with a .45 revolver and went with the Frenchman who drove the lorry at my request to the garage of the Queen's Hotel, Guildhall Street. It was open all night with the attendant, an ex-Royal Navy man, in charge.

"There was only one entrance, and to conceal the lorry all other vehicles were removed to enable the lorry to be put at the back and then surrounded by customers' cars as a kind of protective barrier. I seated myself in the driver's cab

31

Taken on 29th October 1940 at 1,300 feet, from an RAF reconnaisance aircraft, this photograph shows the Folkestone Mill Point Battery position of four 5.5-inch naval guns, formerly the armaments of HMS *Hood*, installed on The Leas in front of Clifton Crescent.

with the .45 pistol close at hand ready for any emergency. Happily nothing untoward happened and I was relieved in the morning as arranged. Later, I asked what the lorry contained. GOLD! — was the reply."

From the Chief Air Raid Warden's Office, dated 3rd November 1943 there is the following: "134 enemy aliens detected at port search and conveyed by Folkestone police to appropriate prisons." (May and June 1940)

***Monday 27th May.** "Operation Dynamo".*

As great and tense a drama as any to beset our island history was soon to take place and has since become known as the "Miracle of Dunkirk".

The evacuation of the British and Allied Armies from French soil, under the command of Admiral Sir Bertram Ramsey, began at dawn on the 27th May, and finished in the late afternoon of June 4th.

The British Expeditionary Force (BEF) waded into the sea at La Panne Sands and at Dunkirk, after the German Army Divisions had moved swiftly into their flanks, effectively severing it from all communications, food and vital supplies. Over 35,000 Allied troops were landed at Folkestone from Royal Navy ships, ferry boats, fishing trawlers and various other but smaller craft. The colossal task of sorting the men into groups relied heavily upon the shoulders of the WVS, Red Cross, Salvation Army and teams of nurses and hundreds of volunteers.

Gallons of tea and thousands of sandwiches were dispensed to the bedraggled, tired and, sometimes, disorientated troops. The majority were then

The four 5.5-inch guns seen here were formerly the armaments of HMS *Hood* before she was refitted and sent to the Far East. The guns were installed on The Leas, opposite Clifton Crescent, and were the responsibility of 412 Battery, RA, part of 550 Coast Defence Battery. The photograph was taken on 30th August 1941, by Lieutenant Tanner.   (I.W.M.)

put on trains which slowly climbed the 1 in 30 gradient up to the Junction Station, where they were shunted onto the main line to London. In all, 64 trains were allotted to Folkestone for the evacuation, and in the nine days it took to evacuate the beaches at Dunkirk, a total of 338,000 British and Allied troops were brought back to these shores.

Friday 31st May. *First invasion threat.*

Plans to counter any invasion threat by Hitler included an order that all signposts throughout the county be taken down, all milestones were to be uprooted and the names of all streets, roads and railway stations obliterated.

Wednesday 5th June. *The stragglers.*

A French fishing boat reached Folkestone with 25 French officers and men on board.

The Mill Point Battery Observation Post was built on the edge of The Leas path at the end of Earls Avenue. Clifton Crescent can be seen on the left of the picture. On 5th October 1940 five civilian workmen were killed here in a concrete shelter.

One of three 8-inch Land Service Guns installed at Capel Le Ferne, near the Valiant Sailor Inn. Electrically powered, they had a dual role in combining a high altitude, anti-aircraft mode with that of Channel defence. The Capel Battery was late both in preparation and construction and did not report "ready for action" until June 1942.

Saturday 8th June. *Aliens — a new order.*

After the traumas of Dunkirk had died down the Mayor of Folkestone gave a "Keep Calm" plea to the townspeople.

In the first week of June, a new order prohibited aliens from residing within 20 miles of certain parts of the coast. A large number of Folkestone's alien population received instructions from the police to move out. Nearly 150 were affected and among these were foreigners who had resided in the town for upwards of 45 years.

In direct contrast the Folkestone Pigeon Federated Club managed to liberate their birds at 8.15 am at Penzance, Cornwall, just before an order was issued that Peregrine Falcons were to be destroyed. For long a protected bird (there were a couple of nesting pairs in the Warren), it was known that Peregrines would "take" a pigeon in flight. The official view was that a pigeon released by a pilot in distress over the sea would meet disaster.

Wednesday 19th June. *0300 hrs — UXHE — District affected — The Warren. Damage nil. Casualties nil.*

The Home Security Intelligence Summary No.580 records that between 1800 hrs on the 18th and 0600 hrs on the 19th the first full-scale air attack on Great Britain occurred. About 100 enemy aircraft crossed the coast of Britain and dropped their bombs almost at random. One of them fell on open land at the Warren. It was not only the first bomb to drop on Folkestone since the First World War, but it failed to explode, and failed to appear in the Intelligence Summary! Somewhere in Kent searchlights probed the night sky and distant ack-ack guns fired a few shells. But one official document states blandly: "There are no AA guns in the Folkestone area".

Bombs and other missiles dropped on Folkestone were principally of the high explosive type used by Germany throughout their assault on the UK mainland. The SC (Sprengbombe-Cylindrisch) was a thin-cased general purpose bomb sometimes called Minenbomben. It had a high charge for maximum blast effect and contained over 50 per cent explosive, used mainly for demolition. Published sources state that eight out of ten HE (high explosive) bombs dropped on the UK were of the SC type, of between 50 and 2,000 kg. A device called the "Trumpets of Jericho" was sometimes fitted to the SC type which was either made from thick cardboard or discarded bayonet scabbards. Approximately 14 inches in length they were shaped like organ pipes and as the bomb fell, the wind blew through the tubes causing them to shriek. This screaming device caused the greatest distress and fear in the civilian population and was designed to undermine their morale.

The SD range (Sprengbombe-Dickwandig), also called Splitterbombe, were designed as either an anti-personnel or semi-armour piercing, with a loading of about 35 per cent explosive. The fragmentation effect was more efficient than the SC although it possessed greater penetration ability due to its streamlined casing.

By June 1940 Hitler's Luftwaffe was making incursions over the British Isles almost unheeded. In the following month our coastal defences were being criticized as paltry. First World War veterans said openly: ". . . barbed wire never stopped anyone". Had Hitler invaded, the 17th Infantry Division would have made their assault along Sandgate Esplanade, well away from the anti-invasion guns sited above the harbour and on The Leas. Above: the deserted Sandgate Esplanade with its meagre line of defence barbed wire. Anti-personnel mines were layed between the groynes.　　　　　　　(I.W.M.)

The armour-piercing PC (Panzerbombe-Cylindrisch) were usually, because of their heavy hardened cast steel casings, used against shipping targets or fortified buildings such as concrete gun emplacements. The explosive loading factor was only about 20 per cent.

One of the most devastating weapons used by Germany, especially when dropped on land targets, was the aerial mine (Luftmine). Originally designed for coastal waters and shipping lanes, it was attached to a parachute and was often used against land targets. With their high charge ratio of between 60 and 70 per cent explosive, the land mine, as they became known to the British, caused considerable blast damage over a very wide area.

Last but by no means least was the incendiary bomb (Brandbombe) which was by far the most damaging weapon used by any air force. They were usually of the 1 and 2 kg magnesium type, each having a thermite filling which burned sufficiently to melt steel. One investigation revealed that one ton of incendiaries could devastate over three acres against only half that area if HEs had been used. Incendiaries were dropped from aircraft in large containers, blown open at a predetermined height by an air-burst fuze, releasing hundreds of missiles over a wide area.

There was a larger type of incendiary similar in appearance to the SC, but not widely used. We called them "fire-pots" and they ranged in size from 50 kg phosphorous-filled Sprengbrand to the 250 and 500 kg oil-filled Flammbombe.

Anderson Shelters were first issued in Folkestone on 1st June 1940. They were designed as a cheap method of family protection from blast and shrapnel. During heavy shelling of the town families spent more than 48 hours in them.

Sunday 23rd June. *School children left town for Wales.*

Plans to counter any invasion threat by Hitler were already being implemented. The first meagre line of defence had already gone up: temporary road barricades around the town. By and large they consisted of disused farm implements such as ploughs, harrows, rollers and carts, with one or two steam traction engines and road rollers and anything else the local authorities could lay their hands on. Eventually these make-shift barriers were replaced by the more permanent concrete structures. Beach areas were cordoned off from the public by rolls of barbed wire entanglements, in front of which were planted hundreds of anti-personnel land mines.

Concrete pillboxes and machine-gun emplacements appeared almost everywhere, some of them cleverly disguised as bathing huts, petrol stations, cafés and kiosks. Old railway track was sunk into the beaches below the water line and was festooned with hundreds more anti-personnel mines.

The whole became, more or less, a barrier against landing craft, although in reality it would have been blown up with ease had invasion forces struck. Nevertheless, it induced confidence in the civilian population, who were required to negotiate the concrete anti-tank blocks called "Dragon's Teeth", erected across the town from Castle Hill Avenue, through Radnor Park and up to Caesars Camp. The Downs which overlook the town still bear the white scars which formed the tank traps, cut out of pure chalk by gangs of men with shovel and spade.

Tuesday 25th June. *Commando raid from Folkestone.*

In the early hours a small party of British Commandos set out from Folkestone in high-speed launches. Other groups were also similarly engaged at Dover and Newhaven. With blackened faces and armed with tommy-guns they slipped out

With the scarred Castle Hill in the background the Cheriton Road Sports Ground is host to the ARP ambulances stationed there during the war years. The requisitioned vehicles, among them Chryslers, Humbers, Ford V8s and Austins, were modified by Martin Walter Ltd; their premises stood close by and now the site of Safeway.

of the harbour to make their daring assault upon the unsuspecting Germans near Boulogne Harbour. One group ran down a German seaplane in the harbour before reaching their destination. Planned as a reconnaissance operation they were to bring back first-hand information of any invasion build-up. Still flushed with the sense of excitement the commandos returned to Folkestone only to find their entry to the inner harbour was challenged by a sentry who asked for the password. The launch stood-off from the quayside for several hours because no one could prove their identity!

However bizarre the commando raid seemed to be, a German invasion attempt on this island became a reality. Hitler's powerful Panzer Divisions were now poised to strike in our direction. Our line of defence spread out between the Isle of Sheppey to Rye in Sussex, under the wing of an ill-equipped 1st London Division, who could only muster about eleven 25 pounder field guns, hardly any anti-tank weapons and about two dozen Bren-Gun Carrier vehicles.

Winston Churchill had said: "I expect the Battle of Britain to begin." It was an astute prediction. Very soon we were to see intense aerial battles fought over Kent, battles fought with individual courage by fighter pilots of both air forces and who acted out a play with a cast of thousands.

Tuesday 2nd July. *German air assault upon Great Britain.*

On July 2nd the German Air Force Supreme Command issued orders in respect of the air onslaught upon Great Britain. From that day small bomber groups, escorted by fighters, roamed over the English Channel areas and made tentative raids upon coastal towns.

Folkestone air raid sirens began sounding almost every day and townspeople were observing more frequently the enemy bomber formations. Occasionally they would stand in groups at street corners to watch the dog-fights high in the blue sky above the town. They would dash indoors as spent cartridge cases and pieces of shrapnel fell around them. During those early days of war it was not uncommon to see the butcher, bank clerk, grocer or baker wearing a fawn coloured arm-band on which were emblazoned the letters LDV or ARP. A tin-hat and gas-mask were never far away either.

Above Folkestone stood RAF Hawkinge, a fighter airfield in existence since the First World War. It was selected as a "Front-Line" airfield within No.11 Group, Fighter Command.

For over twenty years Folkestonians had watched with pride the development of the RAF. Invitations to visit the old aerodrome and take part in the annual "Open Days" had been a feature of peace-time sociability. But now the townspeople were no longer asked to visit "their" aerodrome. All roads leading to it were manned by sentries with fixed bayonets. Concrete pillboxes guarded the high ground. Anti-aircraft guns were sited strategically along the Downs. Also strategically sited were containers filled with petrol, embedded beside roads and lanes. In the event of an invasion petrol would flow out over the roads to be ignited by a well-aimed grenade or Verey-Light cartridge.

Friday 5th July. *Heinkel shot down near Folkestone.*

On the 5th there was another topic of conversation other than the weather. It was just after 6 am when a Heinkel bomber, being harassed by a couple of Spitfires, flew low over the town, trying desperately to reach its French base. People were just rising from their beds when they heard the chatter of machine-gun fire. One eye witness at Capel le Ferne opened her window to see more clearly. She watched the stricken bomber lose height and then disappear from view behind the cliffs. The Heinkel dived into the sea near Lydden Spout. Two crew members swam ashore into the arms of a jubilant AA crew, who had run, helter-skelter, down the steep cliff paths to make their capture. They were Oberfw H. Frischmuth and Uffz R. Marcklovitz, both of whom had been injured. Gefr F. Burger and Gefr F. Martinek were killed and were recovered from the sea later. They are buried at Hawkinge Cemetery.

Saturday 6th July. *0520 hrs — HEs — District affected — Wear Bay Crescent — Hasborough Road — Folkestone Sanatorium. Sanatorium badly damaged — 263 houses slightly damaged. Casualties 1 male injured, 1 female seriously injured, 1 female slightly injured.*

"They've bombed the hospital!" The news spread round the town like wildfire. The sanatorium was only about 300 yards from the Junction Station, which

FOLKESTONE BOROUGH POLICE

THE DUTIES OF CIVILIANS UNDER INVASION CONDITIONS

If invasion occurs before the Government have time to carry out Evacuation plans, everybody in Folkestone will be required to remain. This step is necessary to prevent refugee problems being added to the inevitable difficulties and dangers of invasion, and also to safeguard the people themselves under modern fighting conditions.

It may also be necessary to turn people out of their houses if the latter are situated in defence areas, and if the Military situation requires it. The Police will find suitable accommodation elsewhere in Folkestone for the inhabitants of such houses, should the contingency arise.

WATER. At a given signal, water supplies from the mains will be turned off. You will have VERY SHORT NOTICE of the intention to do this, and you must IMMEDIATELY fill tanks, baths, buckets and every other available receptacle. Water will then only be available at certain points, and the Police and Air Raid Wardens will inform you as to how, and from where your supplies are to be obtained. In some districts the public will be expected to carry water in their own receptacles from an emergency source to their houses, while other districts, namely those which are too far from a source of supply, will be supplied by a mobile tank.

WATER WILL BE STRICTLY RATIONED TO A MAXIMUM OF TWO GALLONS PER HEAD PER DAY.

ALL WATER USED FOR DRINKING PURPOSES DURING THE PERIOD OF EMERGENCY MUST BE BOILED BEFORE USE.

DRAINAGE. After water supplies from the mains are discontinued, WATER CLOSETS MUST NOT BE USED, as water for flushing cannot be distributed.

Foul matter must be buried at least 18 inches deep in the garden.

For those who have no garden, arrangements have been made for the removal of foul matter.

FOOD. Arrangements have been made to ensure your food supply, but if you can afford it a reserve stock of food to LAST SEVEN DAYS should always be kept in stock. When ordered to shelter you must take a supply to last 48 hours.

SHELTER. When you are ordered to take shelter you will be assisted by Police and Air Raid Wardens.

YOU WILL USE YOUR ANDERSON, MORRISON, PROTECTED ROOM, OR OTHER TYPE OF DOMESTIC SHELTER, IF ONE HAS BEEN CONSTRUCTED AT YOUR ADDRESS. ACCOMMODATION WILL NOT BE AVAILABLE FOR YOU IN A PUBLIC SHELTER, IF YOU HAVE A DOMESTIC SHELTER.

The Official Shelter for...

is   ....

This part to be completed by the Officer serving the Notice.

Address at which Notice served...

Number of persons in Household (including children).......................................

Is there a Domestic Shelter for the occupants...

had been the target. It was the first actual air raid made on the town and there is no record of an Alert having been sounded. The first that anyone knew was hearing the scream of the bombs as they fell. One exploded on the tennis court while others demolished the side of one block of wards. Inside were the matron and over a dozen nurses who were in their beds.

When they heard the first bomb fall they ran out into a corridor in their night clothes. Huddled against some sandbags they were showered with glass splinters and falling plaster from the walls and ceilings. When the dust had finally settled they peered over the rubble to see part of their sanatorium in shambles. The blast effect had blown out every window pane in nearby houses. Casualties, however, were very light, largely because most of the patients had been moved out a few days before. The most serious injury happened to Mrs Lillian Allen, an ARP warden, who lost an eye when the windows of her house at 91 Warren Road, blew inwards.

Monday 8th July. *1912 hrs — Machine-gunning — District affected — Black Bull Road — Walton Road — Dawson Road — Bournemouth Road. Casualties 1 female killed.*

When Messerschmitt fighters were making their lightning machine-gun attacks along the coast they were intercepted by Spitfires and Hurricanes who had scrambled from nearby airfields. A number of dog-fights took place at very low level right over the town. Bullets, cartridge cases and all manner of debris fell everywhere. Thirty-six-year-old Miss Elsie Elizabeth Howland was washing up at the kitchen sink at 52 Bournemouth Road, and became Folkestone's first fatality of the war when she was killed instantly by a stray bullet.

By the middle of July a curfew had been imposed under the Defence Regulations Act, which further restricted people living in sensitive areas. It prohibited their movements outside their homes between half an hour before sunset and half an hour before sunrise, unless they had police permission. Spy mania was still around.

In the 'Reynolds News', dated 19th May 1940, George Darling named several well-known members of the Anglo-German Association and a similar organisation called The Link. The latter was reputed to be the most outspoken pro-Nazi organisation in Great Britain. Under Section 18b of the Apprehension of Aliens Act, two prominent members of The Link, who had resided not far from Folkestone, were arrested in London, on Friday 19th July.

Sunday 14th July. *Winston Churchill speaks to nation.*

In the course of his broadcast Churchill said: "Should the invader come, there will be no placid lying down of the people in submission before him as we have seen — alas! — in other countries. We shall defend every village, every town and every city."

Saturday 27th July. Letter to 'Folkestone Herald'.

"Sir,

"The following is the opening paragraph of the Holy Trinity Magazine for July: 'The flood of false rumour about evacuation has been successful in depopulating the town without the expense to the authorities, and in ruining several of the businessmen.'

"This is a very serious statement but unfortunately only too true. Today most of the shops and institutions are closed, and the few businesses which remain open are being run at a loss and unless the population returns will also have to close down.

"Why ruin our beautiful town?.

"Who expects Folkestone to be bombarded or invaded?

"The former would take months to prepare on the French coast and would have to be done secretly without the watchful eye of the RAF detecting it. What a task! The latter would require hundreds of barges or scores of transports and a concentration of tens of thousands of men to have a chance of success.

"The plans of the enemy are to fly over the coast towns very high and to get as far as possible into the country without being heard and causing an alarm to be given — hence our immunity from attack.

"Many people who have been persuaded to leave Folkestone for safety areas have in fact gone into dangerous areas, and suffered more casualties than those who remain here. Folkestone has not suffered serious damage in this war. I make this statement because the daily newspapers so often say "South-East England" or "South-East Coast", in referring to enemy attacks by air.

"I consider the action of the authorities most illogical. The Prime Minister in his broadcast last week referrred to 1941 and perhaps 1942. Are our residents going to stay away from their comfortable homes and beautiful gardens for years?

"What a wonderful summer they have missed, three consecutive months of unbroken sunshine. We cannot remember such a summer, and lovely Folkestone has looked its best. So far as night warnings are concerned, I have not lost a wink of sleep thus far. I may be wrong, I may be mistaken, but I cannot see why Folkestone should be financially ruined and other towns fatten at Folkestone's expense."

Signed: Councillor R.G. Wood

August 1940

In order to establish the necessary conditions for the final conquest of England I intend to intensify air and sea warfare against the English homeland. I therefore order as follows:

1. The Luftwaffe is to overpower the English Air Force with all the forces at its command, in the shortest possible time. The attacks are to be directed primarily against flying units, their ground installations, and their supply organisations, but also against the aircraft industry, including that manufacturing anti-aircraft equipment.

2. After achieving temporary or local air superiority the air war is to be continued against ports, in particular against stores of food, and also against stores of provisions in the interior of the country. Attacks on south coast ports will be made on the smallest possible scale, in view of our own forthcoming operations.

3. On the other hand, air attacks on enemy warships and merchant ships may be reduced except where some particularly favourable target happens to present itself, where such attacks would lend additional effectiveness to those mentioned in paragraph 2, or where such attacks are necessary for the training of aircrews for further operations.

4. The intensified air warfare will be carried out in such a way that the Luftwaffe can at any time be called upon to give adequate support to naval operations against suitable targets. It must also be ready to take part in full force in "Undertaking Sea Lion".

5. I reserve to myself the right to decide on terror attacks as measures of reprisal.

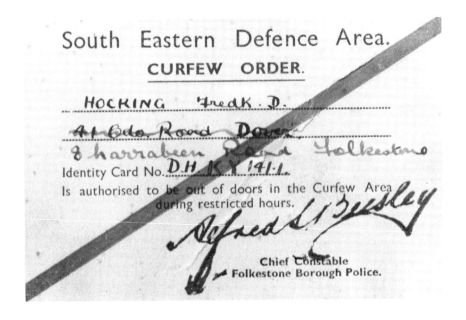

South Eastern Defence Area.

CURFEW ORDER.

HOCKING   Fredk. D.

41 Bdo Road Dover

8 harrabeen Road Folkestone

Identity Card No. DH 15 X 141-1

Is authorised to be out of doors in the Curfew Area
during restricted hours.

Alfred L. Beesley

Chief Constable
Folkestone Borough Police.

6. The intensification of the air war may begin on or after August 5. The exact
time is to be decided by the Luftwaffe after the completion of preparations
and in the light of the weather. The Kriegsmarine is authorised to begin the
proposed intensified naval war at the same time.
ADOLF HITLER, DIRECTIVE No. 17, AUGUST 1, 1940

Saturday 10th August. *LDV plea for bedding.*
This was a plea in the local newspaper from the LDV units in and around the
town for beds, bedding and old wireless sets. It was in August that the Prime
Minister, Mr Winston Churchill, changed the name of the volunteer units from
LDV to the Home Guard. The plea pointed out that those who had finished their
"stint" at sentry duty needed to lay their heads down somewhere in relative
comfort.

Sid Lester was a member of "Dad's Army", as it was dubbed after the war. He
had joined the Folkestone Gasworks Platoon, and recalls: "At first we guarded
the gasworks where I worked with pick-axe handles, but we were soon properly
organised with guns. Even the de-greasing plant, used to clean the old black
cookers, came in useful to clean up the rifles which were shipped over from the
USA. We in the gasworks units would be out on Hythe ranges on Sundays, or
practising with machine guns at the brickfields near Caesar's Camp."

Another eyewitness, Eric Hart, remembers: "Finally when all the frenzied
activity had died down after Dunkirk the harbour fell silent and was deserted

except for the lone tramp steamer which was positioned at the mouth of the harbour, with its bows close to the lighthouse and its stern reaching back towards the East Cliff Sands. The sea-cocks were then opened and the black funnelled ship slowly settled on the bottom for the purpose of denying the enemy the port facilities.

"The large steel doors, leading out to the outer jetties were set in concrete. The swing-bridge, which carried the railway to the harbour, was swung open halfway then concrete was poured into the machinery."

"Boffins thought up so many ingenious ruses to fool the enemy that we were bristling with defences," recalls Eric Hart, ". . . One of them was setting up telegraph poles along the coastline, erected in the near horizontal and pointing out to sea with camouflage netting draped over the rear ends surrounded by sandbags. Even some of the townspeople were misled by this dummy artillery."

And then there were the rumours which spread around the town like wildfire. One of them concerned the Victoria Pier. A contingent of sappers was about to blow it up.

"People turned up to see this spectacle but were prevented from getting too close," recalls Eric Hart, ". . . everyone became excited as the official time drew near to blow the old pier to simthereens. But everyone was dismayed when they heard just a mild 'crack' and, instead of seeing the whole structure disappearing into the vertical with an accompanying 'whoosh', just a small section of the pier promenade fell onto the beach. The whole structure seaward remained intact, and so did a large hoarding which proclaimed 'Dancing 'till Midnight'."

Monday 12th August. *1045 to 1137 hrs — Shelling — District affected — Millfield — Cornwallis Avenue — Shorncliffe Road — Danton Pinch. 1 house destroyed, 1 house partly destroyed, 30 houses damaged. Casualties 1 male injured.*

On 12th August, which dawned fine and clear, the Luftwaffe prepared to attack targets in Southern England. Soon after first light the "free-chase" Messerschmitt fighters were sent over Kent. The bombers came over in force later to knock-out the radar installations along our coastline, and to smash the "front-line" fighter stations.

At 10.45 am the first bombardment of Folkestone began when the German long-range guns opened fire. It is almost certain that the first shells to reach the town came from the K5 — 280 mm Railway Guns, capable of firing a 561 lb shell over 38 miles. These massive artillery pieces were then operating on French railway track between Wimereux and Marquise.

The first shell hit 14 Millfield, where Mrs Stone had lived before she was evacuated further inland. Had she been there she might not have reached her 100th birthday. The next shell exploded in Cornwallis Avenue partially demolishing a house, and the third damaged the home of Police Sergeant Rowe, in Shorncliffe Road. The fourth and last shell of the salvo fell on open ground at Danton Pinch.

Several large saloon cars were cannibalised to supplement the pitiful shortage of ambulances in the area. Above — a modified Dodge saloon attached to "C" Group ARP Post at Baker Road, Cheriton.

The Baker Road ARP Warden's Post, Cheriton, being cleared of snow in the winter of 1940. The post doubled as First Aid Post No.4 — other First Aid Posts were No.1 Royal Victoria Hospital; No.2 The Salvation Army HQ, Bradstone Road; No.3 Chichester Hall, Sandgate, and No.5 Sports Ground, Cheriton Road.

1807 hrs — HEs & IBs — District affected — Garden Road — Walton Road — Albert Road — Wingate Road — Harvey Place — Black Bull Road — Canterbury Road — Folly Road — Morrison Road — Dawson Road — Linden Crescent — Fernbank Crescent — East Street — Myrtle Road — Edward Road — Burrow Road — Golf Links.

It was shortly after 5.30 pm when a formation of Junkers 88 bombers were plotted on radar. Approaching Dymchurch it split into two separate groups, one made for Lympne airfield while the other turned towards RAF Hawkinge. Within just a few terrifying minutes, the airfield and village of Hawkinge, and nearby areas of Folkestone, were to experience the detonations of high explosive bombs and fires started by incendiaries.

Buildings collapsed with deafening intensity, doors and windows were blown out, roofs caved-in and trees were uprooted. A second wave of bombers came in and were met by anti-aircraft shells from 3-inch heavy ack-ack batteries in the area. Although it was hoped in the early stages of the war that deception would play a major part in the defence of the British Isles, the Folkestone Golf Links was never intended to be a fake or dummy aerodrome. A fake airfield was later constructed at Wooten but it never deceived the Luftwaffe. The second wave of bombers released their bombs and incendiaries on the golf links.

It was not a navigational error. Over 90 bombs fell in a line from the bottom of Waterworks Hill, across the golf links to the western end of Mead Road. Grazing sheep were flung into the air grotesquely. Eight died and many were injured.

Sid Lester recalls: "I watched a group of bombers peeling off out of their formation and systematically bomb what they must have thought was Hawkinge aerodrome. In fact it was the golf links. Two bombs dropped within yards of where I was standing in the back garden of a house in Garden Road. As the planes turned I hopped over the garden wall and dived into my neighbour's Anderson Shelter. The next thing I knew there was rubble filling-up the entrance from the house behind in Walton Road. There in the middle of the wreckage was a bloke standing, his face black with dust. "Crumbs! — are you all right?" I asked. Meanwhile, in front of the house another bomb had exploded in clay subsoil. A great plug of clay had blown up into the air and had come down through my roof!"

Two bombs straddled 26 and 28 Linden Crescent, where several people had taken shelter in their garden Anderson. The blast shook them up like sardines in a tin can but no one was hurt. When an incendiary fell through the roof at 10 Wingate Road, dozens of buckets and tin baths appeared suddenly from nowhere and a human chain was soon organised without anyone giving a second's thought.

Wardens, policemen and firemen were numbed by the multiple calls but there was no panic. Time was the precious commodity and, as often happens in emergencies, there were feelings of exhilaration.

This particular section of the Victoria Pier was demolished in 1940 as part of the defence measures against invasion. The span was blown up by sappers of the REME and can be seen lying on the beach. In 1943 the static water tanks erected in the town were being filled with sea water, pumped up from the pier by a borehole pump installed in the Pier Pavilion. A scaffold bridge was erected over the missing span. (Kent Fire Brigade)

The incident board in the Control Centre was crammed with chalked information — 16 Harcourt Road roof damage — 14 Dawson Road roof damage — 6 & 8 Fernbank Crescent badly damaged — 11 Myrtle Road incendiary alight — 32 Canterbury Road incendiary in attic — 35 Burrow Road incendiary in roof — UXB (unexploded bomb) in Morrison Road — 1 Harvey Place incendiary in attic — 62 Black Bull Road badly damaged by bomb — 62 Garden Road badly damaged by bomb — 57 Walton Road 1 male trapped — 25 Albert Road badly damaged by bomb — 4 Victoria Road incendiary in attic.

In the evening dozens of hand carts were observed, stacked high with furniture, carpets and caged birds, trundling from one street to another. A Black Bull Road shopkeeper was painting his heavily-scarred shutters.

Tuesday 13th August. *Hitler's main plan of air attack known as Adlerangriff (Attack of the Eagles), came into operation on this day and code-named Adler Tag (Eagle Day).*

After the previous day's events Folkestone experienced more air activity. Dorniers, Heinkels and Messerschmitts were scurrying back towards the French coast, many of them being followed by Hurricanes and Spitfires. One German fighter had caught alight and crashed into a field at Denton. The pilot, Uffz H. Wemhoner, had baled out and landed heavily in a field near Henbury, where Mrs Betty Tylee and her friend Miss Jean Smitherson found him with a broken leg.

"He thought he was going to be shot," said Mrs Tylee, "but I told him we did not do that kind of thing."

Although in considerable pain Wemhoner's chief concern was for his flying helmet which carried a talisman.

"He asked us in what country he was."

Two soldiers arrived shortly afterwards and they carried him to the nearby farmhouse where Mrs Ash said later: "He thanked me for the cup of tea in perfect English."

The farmer and his young son had been reaping in an adjoining field when the burning Messerschmitt had narrowly missed them before plunging into the ground. Hans Wemhoner apologised and said he had no alternative!

Wednesday 14th August. *Stuka dive-bomber shot down.*

Dog-fights were going on in the Folkestone area and a number of Stuka JU87Bs were trying to fight off the persistent RAF fighters. Eyewitnesses saw one Stuka shot down which crashed into the sea while another, badly damaged, limped over the waves with most of its tail section in ribbons.

Thursday 15th August. *1150 hrs — 3 planes crashed. District affected — Shorn-cliffe Crescent — Northcliffe House — Danton Pinch. 3 houses seriously damaged, 5 houses slightly damaged. Casualties 10 male injured, 2 female injured.*

Luftwaffe reconnaissance flights set off the "Alert" sirens very early. They were to set the scene for Folkestone to experience some of the bold air attacks aimed at British defences. The townspeople were now used to hearing the peculiar, deep throbbing noises made by aero-engines, a phenomena caused by different engines becoming almost synchronised. They were also becoming used to hearing the thin cry of the hand-operated siren. "It was . . ." as one local journalist wrote, ". . . an academic sort of second fiddle to the more robust, electrically-operated sirens to which we had become accustomed."

This Thursday broke fine and warm and there was just a trace of haze over the English Channel. By about 11 am a huge armada of over sixty Stuka dive-bombers, heavily escorted by the incomparable Messerschmitt fighters, left their French bases to attack RAF coastal aerodromes.

When the bombs and incendiaries crashed down on Hawkinge the raiders were, in turn, set upon by our own fighters. The terrible screaming noises of the Stukas, the bursting bombs, the rattle of machine-guns and the sound of anti-aircraft guns firing in quick succession was enough to put fear into the hearts of many who experienced it.

Harold Knight recalled: ". . . many of the town's building trade were out of work. One day we were told to assemble at the Labour Exchange. We were taken to Shorncliffe Camp and were issued with pick-axe and shovel and then taken to the hills above Holy Well. We had to hew a tank trap about 15 feet drop, 7 feet wide, out of solid chalk. To me, and no doubt to many others, this was sacrilege to my childhood playground. I remember the wild flowers — the bee

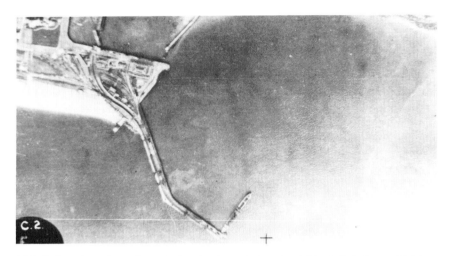

Hitler's invasion plans showed that he intended to land his 17th Infantry Division between Hythe and Sandgate, and then move inland and behind Folkestone to take the harbour. Naval mines had been sunk in a line from the stern of the blockship to Copt Point, and would have been released from their cradles, electrically operated from the Naval OP, situated on top of Martello Tower No.3. Above: the steamship s.s. *Umvoti*, 3,217 tonnes, built in 1903 at Whiteinch, arrived at Folkestone on 29th July 1940. The 419-feet, single-funnel tramp steamer was scuttled at the Southern Railway pier-head. This aerial photograph was taken by an RAF reconnaisance aircraft on 6th August 1940.

(John Guy)

orchids, cowslips, harebells, daisies and scabious. I remembered too the myriad butterflies and from that day those beautiful hills behind Folkestone were never as beautiful as they were prior to our handywork.

"We had neither drinking water nor toilets — but many blisters! As we got round to Caesar's Camp we saw many dog-fights. We used to bolt for the trees at the bottom of Sugar Loaf Hill for cover. We had a bird's-eye view of what was going on. We saw planes going down into the sea and some of them flew right over our heads. We cowered at the bottom of one trench. I have never been so scared in all my life!"

1535 hrs — HEs — District affected — Prospect Place — Sandgate — Weymouth Road — Shaftsbury Avenue. 2 houses demolished, 17 houses seriously damaged, 4 houses slightly damaged. Casualties nil.

Beneath the dog-fights, bullets and anti-aircraft shells fell into the streets. Mr Taylor, standing behind the counter in his chemist shop at 31 Cheriton High Street, crouched instinctively as several bullets neatly pierced the plate-glass window. The bullets presumably came from a Hurricane which had given a "coup-de-grace" burst, aimed at a low-flying Stuka. The stricken dive-bomber

50

seared through the electric power lines at Morehall sub-station, and then spun into houses in Shorncliffe Crescent. The pilot, Uffz Hermann Weber, was burned to a cinder. The gunner, Uffz Franz Kraus, had managed to bale out. Kraus was later found severely wounded by Mrs Oram and Gordon Botsford, outside 81 Harcourt Road. Mrs Macdonald, who lived close by, ran out to give first aid before the unfortunate gunner was taken to the Royal Victoria Hospital. Kraus died three days later.

A warden's report states that two 250-kilo bombs were still in their bomb-racks beneath the wings, but another report indicates a single 500-kilo bomb failed to explode on impact and was found later lodged in the front bedroom of 83 Shorncliffe Crescent.

Police Constable Crane was sent to Folkestone Hospital later that afternoon to obtain particulars of the gunner's identity. While searching his clothing he found a letter from the gunner's girlfriend who had expressed her fear for him when she learned he was flying over England!

In a damaged, semi-detached suburban house, 80 Shorncliffe Crescent, were Mrs Wheelan and Miss Morgan. The rescue party were told by Miss Morgan: "We were just preparing to go out shopping when the raid began. It seemed so close we thought it better to stay indoors. We took shelter in the cupboard under the stairs. Suddenly there was a terrific crash and the house absolutely rocked. We remained in the cupboard until we heard someone shouting. When we went out we saw the wrecked German plane which was still smouldering. Afterwards one of the crew was found burned to death in the cockpit."

In the evening, PC Crane was on duty in Cheriton when he heard ". . . the incessant hub-hub in the sky above." With another constable they watched a Hurricane, obviously damaged, making for an area where there were anti-glider posts erected. "We made haste on our cycles to get there and endeavoured to warn the pilot by frantic waving of our arms. He managed to land his machine without any further damage."

Sub-Lieutenant H.W. Beggs of 151 Squadron had tangled with a Messerschmitt over Dover at about 7.15 pm. PC Crane and his companion lifted the wounded pilot from the cockpit. His face was bleeding from a cut and there were bullet wounds in his right shoulder and left thigh. He had little idea where he had landed, and when told Folkestone he showed relief. As they carried him to the ambulance he said: "There are thousands of the bastards up there!"

PC Crane recalled another British fighter which had come down just behind the Royal Victoria Hospital. A guard consisting of several young airmen was posted around the aircraft pending its removal.

"At night, if there is too much concentration there is apt to be a tendency to perceive things which are not there. The more one stares into the darkness the more likely is the imagination to play tricks. A guard thought he saw something and shouted 'HALT!' — others caught the nervous tension and began to shout, then a shot was fired. Everybody started shooting into the darkness. The police were called and order was only restored by constables advancing towards the frightened airmen with their torches illuminating their uniforms!"

This photograph of a German long-range gun, which can be seen in the Grace Hill Museum, Folkestone, was actually taken on 12th August 1940 when the first salvo was fired at the town. It is almost certain to be one of the K5 280mm railway guns, capable of firing a 561lb shell for a distance of 38 miles. (Folkestone Museum)

In June 1940 the Auxiliary Fire Service, initially based at the Dover Road Fire Station, was moved in units of eight men, a pump and associated equipment, to specially selected areas in the town. The Leas bandstand was used by one team, seen here in late July 1940: Joe Punnet, Gordon Mordant, Edgar Newman, Section Leader Bauman and Tom Waddup. (E. Newman)

Several Stukas had been shot down and because one of them severed the power lines all the cinema performances in the town were cancelled.

There was another "Alert" sounded at 6.15 pm. The town was strangely quiet. Folkestone was specifically mentioned in the BBC's eight o'clock news broadcast that evening in connection with the series of air raids. To mention Folkestone was quite unusual in a radio broadcast. It was usually referred to as a "South Coast Town".

Because most Anderson Shelters were lit by candlelight there was suddenly a shortage of candles in the town. Nevertheless, overheard in one shelter that day: "My dear, I did half the foot in this morning's raid, I did the rest of the foot in this afternoon's raid, I'm doing the leg now, and if we have another raid tonight then I shall have finished knitting the whole of it in one day!"

Monday 26th August. *1152 hrs — HEs — District affected — Park Farm — Canterbury Road — Darby Road — Darby Place — Darlington Street — Guildhall Street — Brockman Road — Claremont Road — Coolinge Road — Kingsnorth Gardens — Russell Road — Alder Road — Radnor Park Road — Bonsor Road — Watkins Road — Coastguard Cottages — Lower Sandgate Road — Marine Crescent — Marine Parade — Marine Terrace. Salter's Laundry demolished, 6 houses demolished, 53 houses badly damaged, 356 houses slightly damaged. Casualties 5 killed, 24 injured.*

The pattern of the daylight raids over England, now that Herr Goering was concentrating his bombers to wipe out the Royal Air Force, was much the same as all previous raids. Huge bomber formations were flying over the town, heading inland to attack targets closer to London.

Townspeople watched in awe and fascination as dozens of severely damaged bombers struggled back towards France. There was much jubilation when they saw one or two being shot down and even greater excitement when they saw a German dive into the Channel, sending up a plume of spray.

On the 26th, about forty Heinkels and a dozen Dorniers with scores of Messerschmitt fighters crossed the coast near Deal at about 11.30 am, but while the main force flew inland some of them swung west to attack Folkestone. People were still running for shelter when the first bomb screamed towards them.

At Salter's Laundry, Park Farm, a number of staff had no time to seek shelter before the main part of the building received two direct hits. The bodies of three employees were later recovered from the wreckage. Two of the victims were young girls, 17-year-old Louise Hart and 19-year-old Annie Todd. The other victim was 60-year-old Charles Holloway. A number of others were injured, two only being detained in hospital. Fortunately only a skeleton workforce was at the premises, otherwise casualties would have been much higher.

Mrs Christine Nash, who was working in the office of the laundry, said later: "I heard aeroplanes flying very low but thought they were ours until just afterwards there came the scream of bombs. I threw myself forward over my desk to protect my head as best I could and said a little prayer.

"There were then two terrific explosions. I was covered with glass, wood splinters and plaster. When it seemed a little quieter I began to move my arms and legs. Glass had cut me in several places but I eventually managed to crawl out from beneath the debris. As I emerged from the wreckage I could hear machine guns. The thought crossed my mind that they would see me because I was wearing a light blue frock. But then I met rescuers."

The young girls who had been killed had been working in the calender room which received a direct hit. Mr Holloway had been in the washroom. Others working in outbuildings escaped the main force of the explosions, although a former Folkestone footballer, Jimmie Thompson, received cuts to his head.

All that remained of the Stuka dive-bomber which was shot down on 15th August 1940 whilst attempting to attack RAF Hawkinge. The Ju87B of 10/LG1 struck the high tension wires at Shorncliffe Road and spun into 82–83 Shorncliffe Crescent. Both German airmen were later buried at Folkestone New Cemetery, Hawkinge, where they remain to this day.
(Imperial War Museum)

Eighteen-year-old Miss Ethel Harris, also in the calender room, was eventually rescued without a stitch of clothing on her body. Found beneath a pile of rubble she was quickly wrapped in a sheet. Seriously injured she was immediately taken to hospital.

Houses in the immediate neighbourhood were stripped of their roof tiles and not one pane of glass survived the blast. Almost all the bombs dropped had screamers attached which was frightening to the townspeople who had never before experienced an air raid of such intensity.

On the other side of town a row of houses in Marine Crescent was completely flattened by a stick of high explosive bombs. It resulted in an immense cloud of brick dust which rose in the air above the Royal Pavilion Hotel, carrying with it slates, bricks and splintered woodwork.

Mrs Morrison, living at 16 Lower Sandgate Road, had taken refuge under the stairs. The house collapsed and she was entombed for several hours. Police Constable Spain of the Folkestone Borough Police received an emergency call from the harbour area. He raced to the scene and was told that a woman was trapped in one of the buildings. Whilst the rescue teams moved tons of rubble by hand PC Spain, ignoring the tottering walls which might have fallen at any moment, burrowed into the debris until he reached Mrs Morrison who was pinned down by her legs. Spain elected to stay with her, comforting her until the rescue team could get through. She was not seriously hurt, but when Spain began his first aid routine on one of her hands, she shook it and remarked: "Oh! — don't worry about that — it's plum jam. I must have stuck my hand in it when the bomb fell!"

For his courageous efforts in risking his life to rescue Mrs Morrison, PC William Thomas Elnor Spain was later awarded the George Medal.

One other victim was unaccounted for when a five-storey building collapsed. The body of Mr H. Bishop, a NAAFI manager, was not found until several months later when the site was being cleared.

Thomas Gibson, upholsterer and cabinet maker at 18 Lower Sandgate Road, had a similar experience to Mrs Morrison. He heard the drone of aircraft and decided to go outside to have a closer look. He never reached the front door. The bomb exploded and the blast catapulted him immediately down a flight of stairs to the basement. The house collapsed on top of him. When the rescue teams finally reached him several hours later they found his life had been saved by the very staircase down which he had been blown. The heavy staircase had fallen across him thus protecting him from the mass of wreckage that fell on top.

At the gasworks allotments in Archer Road, 79-year-old George Knight was sitting in his shed when a 1,000-kilo bomb exploded nearby. It made a 20-feet deep crater. George was killed instantly.

Friday 30th August. *1816 hrs — Town machine-gunned. Some slight casualties.*

A terrified dog was running loose in the streets. A local farmer was charging the public a small fee to look at a huge bomb crater in one of his fields. By his enterprise he raised thirty shillings for the Red Cross Fund.

Saturday 31st August. *There had been a flying start to the Spitfire Fund with over £350 collected in the first six days. The ultimate goal was £5,000, the cost of one Spitfire. Collecting boxes appeared in public houses, cinemas and even in air raid shelters.*

Monday 2nd September. *1735 hrs. HEs and oil incendiary — District affected — Folkestone Harbour & Stade — 124 Cheriton Road. Casualties nil.*

On 1st September German shipping began to move from their North Sea ports to the Channel coast. Three days later Hitler had issued orders for the preparation of "Operation Sealion", the code-name for the invasion of England. The earliest date for the invasion fleet landing was fixed for 21st September.

Folkestone Harbour was, undoubtedly, of strategic importance and featured prominently in the invasion plans. Even so, there seemed little advantage if the

The Beresford Pump in the foreground was originally towed by a lorry which was hastily summoned in an emergency. The lorry was owned by a coal merchant and the AFS crew were required to unload it before it could proceed to the incident. The crew are: Dick Rogers, Martin, Harold Jenner, Edgar Newman, Gus Bartelous, Joe and Stan Boorman. After the August 1940 air raids the unit was moved to St Mary's Convent, Shorncliffe Road. (E. Newman)

harbour was also to be featured in heavy bombing raids which might have demolished vital structures.

Nevertheless, on the 2nd an unidentified enemy bomber planted a well-aimed oil-bomb in the harbour and a high explosive bomb near to the Royal Pavilion Hotel. The clock in the hotel tower, already useless from action on 12th August, blew out completely.

The seriously depleted Folkestone fishing fleet, with their fishing grounds hemmed-in by mine-fields, had already been blown up by mines, caught, some of them, in their nets, had been machine-gunned and blamed for showing lights at night! Now their Stade was alight with burning oil, spreading along the quayside like greased lightning. Was this the prelude to invasion? they thought.

The events which happened the following day were, to say the least, rather incredulous. Shortly before five o'clock in the morning on 3rd September, Private Tollervey of the Somerset Light Infantry challenged a man near the sea wall at the Grand Redoubt, West Hythe. Charles van der Kieboom, a 26-year-old Dutchman, was promptly taken to the guardroom where a search revealed he was carrying a loaded pistol. Within half an hour Kieboom's accomplice, Sjord

Pons, another Dutchman, was caught. Later that day a wireless transmitter and associated equipment was found in a nearby field.

Further west, two other spies were landed near Dungeness. They managed to survive twenty-four hours before they, in turn, were captured. Rudolf Waldberg, the only German in the group, was accompanied by Carl Meier, whose origins were never clearly established. They too possessed a transmitter, later found in a tree near the seashore. Meier spoke English well enough not to cause alarm, but his knowledge of the basic English way of life caused his downfall. Long before regular opening hours he walked to a Lydd public house and asked for cider. When he returned later he was arrested by a police sergeant. The police picked up Waldberg on the following day, but not before he had sent three radio messages to his masters in French.

The incompetent foursome, ill-trained and lacking the rudimentary knowledge for survival in a foreign land, were all in custody within thirty-six hours.

In November, they appeared at the Old Bailey for trial. They had been sent to England to find out the strength of our military defences. Pons was acquitted, but the others were hanged in Pentonville Prison.

Wednesday 4th September. *0935 hrs — RAF aeroplane in sea off Folkestone. Pilot machine-gunned.*

During the first week of September RAF losses were running at a higher rate than their German counterparts. But our pilots forced to bale out had the reassurance that they would either land in familiar surroundings or would be plucked from the sea within an hour or two, by rescue craft. Flt Lt Bruce, still strapped in his cockpit, had already gone to a watery grave. For Plt Off Maccinski who took to his parachute when his Hurricane plunged towards the sea off Folkestone, there was no reassurance. Half expecting to see a rescue launch speeding out of the harbour, he saw, instead, a Messerschmitt turning in his direction. Eyewitnesses standing on The Leas were horrified to observe the callousness of the incident. It was so unnecessary. Maccinski was dead before he reached the sea.

Friday 6th September. *1815 hrs — Machine gunning — District affected — Gordon Road, Cheriton. Casualties 1 child killed.*

It was shortly after 6 pm when three Messerschmitts came over the town on what was often called a "free-chase". They machine-gunned streets and houses with no particular target in mind. Officially they were known as "nuisance raids". People ran for the nearest cover and at 4 Gordon Road, Cheriton, Mrs White told Sheila, her nine-year-old daughter, to run to the garden shelter. Her father, Warrant Officer White of the Royal West Kent Regiment, was already a prisoner of war in Germany.

Sheila, hearing the commotion, looked round the shelter door and called her mother. It was at that moment she was struck by a bullet. She died instantly.

Members of the bandstand AFS crew with their Coventry Climax Pump and the requisitioned saloon car used for towing.

Saturday 7th September. *1800 hrs — Messerschmitt Bf109 fighter shot down off Folkestone. Pilot captured.*

This day was the start of the London Blitz. It was just after 11 o'clock in the morning when the Observer Post in the Martello Tower on The Leas spotted through the haze a formation of enemy aircraft. They flew over Sandgate and attacked Hawkinge airfield. For most of the day there was an uncanny silence after that raid. Shortly after 6 o'clock a mass attack was made on London and other cities. There were enemy fighters and bombers everywhere. Flg Off Scott of 41 Squadron brought down an enemy fighter within sight of the seashore. Uffz W. Melchert swam ashore and was captured by waiting troops on the beach.

On the following day the 4th Super-Heavy Railway Battery, Royal Artillery, moved to its operational position during the night. The Right Section gun, named "S.M. Cleeve", went to Hythe railway station while the Left Section gun, named "E.E. Gee", arrived at the sidings east of Folkestone just west of the short tunnel leading to the coastal line to Dover.

On Thursday 12th "E.E. Gee" was visited by the Prime Minister, the Chief of the Imperial General Staff, the First Sea Lord of the Admiralty, the Commander-in-Chief Home Forces and many others. The 9.2-inch gun-crew went through their routine without a hitch, even to the point of putting a live shell in the breach. When the crew stood to attention at their positions there were murmurs of approval from the "Top Brass" but the order "Fire" was not given. The big gun did not go into action until October.

58

Friday 13th September. *1450 hrs — HEs & IBs — District affected — Park Farm Brickfields — Walton Gardens — Downs Road — Golf Links. Damage nil. Casualties nil.*

Monday 23rd September. *1000 hrs — Messerschmitt Bf109 shot down in sea off Folkestone.*

Just after 10 o'clock in the morning an enemy fighter skimmed over the waves close to the dilapidated Victoria Pier. The pilot, Uffz Dilthey, was seen to catapult out of his cockpit when the aircraft hit the sea. Lieutenant M.E. Jacobs, RA, standing on the pier, stripped to his waist and jumped. He swam almost a quarter of a mile before reaching the exhausted pilot, but managed to keep the German afloat until they were picked up by a fishing boat. Dilthey, suffering from a fractured leg and a bullet wound in one shoulder, was eventually and unceremoniously dumped upon the quayside where a small crowd had gathered. They stood and stared at Dilthey in open defiance before he was taken away to the military hospital in the Hotel Metropole.

Thursday 26th September. *1730 hrs — HEs & IBs — District affected — Herdson Road — Welson Road — Baldric Road — Bathurst Road — Coolinge Lane — Turketel Road — Shorncliffe Road — Broadfield Road — 2 houses seriously damaged — 12 houses slightly damaged. Casualties nil.*

This evening raid on the western end of the town resulted in a shower of incendiaries being scattered over a wide area. Fire-fighting teams were called from many districts to help douse the fizzling missiles which had fallen through roofs. Perhaps the most serious damage of all happened at the "Glen Royal" Hotel in Coolinge Lane, where the incendiary canister had fallen.

Friday 27th September. *1145 hrs — HEs — District affected — Payers Park — Holy Trinity Church — 12 houses seriously damaged — 122 houses slightly damaged. Casualties 1 female injured.*

Enemy bombers and fighters had been flying over the town since about 6 am. Townspeople half expected to receive a raid at any moment. The 3-inch anti-aircraft guns of the 1st Heavy AA Regiment Royal Marines, sited above the town behind the Downs, were firing their shells into a clear sky where the bursts indicated the line of flight. But the droning engines continued. Heinkels, Junkers and Messerschmitts were seen over the town in formations numbering hundreds. It was an extraordinary sight. But what was even more extraordinary was to see the enemy aircraft fleeing back towards France, their wings and fuselages damaged and their engines belching out black, oily smoke. RAF Hurricanes and Spitfires were observed flying at varying heights, their chattering machine-guns were applauded by the onlookers who peered out of doorways at a spectacle they would never forget.

Just before noon a Junkers 88 was being attacked by our fighters. The German pilot was heading for the sea in a desperate attempt to evade the determined

A Fire Service Department was first implemented at the Home Office and its reorganisation and standardisation required the new service to be divided into 39 Fire Services. Most of Kent became 30 Fire Force and Folkestone was designated "E" Division, where women were recruited increasingly to act as telephonists and drivers. (Wm Lester)

attacks. The bomb doors opened and the pilot released a single 1,000-kilo bomb, which exploded in a garden at the rear of Holy Trinity Church. Red hot shrapnel seared through masonry while the blast smashed every windowpane within half a mile.

Five minutes later another Junkers jettisoned its bomb load on Payers Park area where a dozen houses had to be evacuated. Considering the resultant damage to the town when over 500 enemy aircraft had been passing overhead it was a miracle that there was only one casualty.

Saturday 28th September. 1720 hrs — HEs — District affected — Folkestone Harbour — Royal Pavilion Hotel — Payers Park. Damage — hotel slightly damaged. Casualties nil.

Sentries in the harbour were sipping mugs of hot tea when anti-aircraft fire was heard in the Dover area. A Bofors gun crew had been fishing. They had been "stood-to" and "stood-down" in a succession of "Alerts", almost continuous since daybreak. A spell of fishing seemed a pleasurable pastime. Now they ran to their gun, leaving their fishing lines dangling over the side of the pier, but before they could don their tin-hats three Junkers 88 bombers were heading towards them at no more than about eight hundred feet. The Bofors was swinging round to bear on the targets when black bomb-cases fell away from the fast, twin-engined aircraft. Because of the low height the 500-kilo bombs skipped and jumped across the harbour walls and buildings. Not one exploded on impact. One in particular bounced off the road in front of the Royal Pavilion Hotel, went through a window, penetrated the basement and came to rest on a pile of carpets.

Another bomb spun round and round like a top coming to rest at the harbour entrance. The whole harbour area was immediately sealed off. Police, both military and civil, stood their distance from the UXBs. The Bomb Disposal Unit at Chatham was summoned. But before they reached Folkestone however, an army officer leaped into a stationary lorry and moved it away from danger. Later, using a stethoscope, a bomb disposal officer discovered two of the bombs were still ticking!

Friday 4th October. *1205 hrs — HEs — District affected — Julian Road — Golf Links — Damage 2 houses seriously damaged, Golf Clubhouse seriously damaged, 19 houses slightly damaged. Casualties nil.*
2 unexploded bombs blew up at 8 pm.

Saturday 5th October. *0942 hrs — HEs & IBs — District affected — open fields near Tile Kiln Lane. Damage nil. Casualties nil.*
This was the first of four attacks made on the town this Saturday morning. A Junkers 88 dropped several bombs and one large incendiary canister on a market garden. Once again Luftwaffe pilots were misled into thinking the Golf Links was in some way connected to Hawkinge airfield.

1059 hrs — HEs — District affected — Varne Place — East Cliff. Damage 5 houses slightly damaged. Casualties nil.
Eyewitness accounts believe the bombs fell short of their target which, presumably, was the guns at Copt Point.

1150 hrs — HEs — District affected — The Leas — Clifton Crescent — Shorncliffe Road. Damage 1 blockhouse destroyed, 38 houses slightly damaged. Casualties 5 male killed, 1 male injured.
Although Hitler had postponed "Operation Sealion" on 17th September until further notice, his bomber formations were still attacking targets on a wide front. Accounts of this particular raid vary as to what type of aircraft was used which scattered bombs between The Leas and Shorncliffe Road. One report gives two high-flying Heinkels while another says they were JU88s. While the purists argue there is little doubt that one of the targets was the Mill Point gun site on The Leas. A direct hit on an uncompleted concrete blockhouse at the end of Earls Avenue was a terrible tragedy. Five men working on the building had taken refuge inside it the moment they heard anti-aircraft fire. The reinforced

By September 1940, despite Hitler's postponement of his invasion plans "Operation Sealion", the Folkestone Borough Police Force was issued with rifles. The police were, at that time, in possession of .45 calibre revolvers, which had been provided under a special emergency department established at the Kent Police HQ, in April 1939. Above: in this picture, taken in 1941, are from left to right: Sergeant Allard; PC Poole; PC McKenzie; PC Osborne; PC Pledgar; PC Crane and PC Budgeon.

concrete was not sufficiently hardened to withstand a direct hit and it collapsed killing William J. Gardner (28), Albert J. Moore (49), Arthur E. Potten (43), Edward R. Hart (36), and William J. Unwin (36), all of them married and working for a local builder.

1335 hrs — HEs — District affected — Wear Bay Road — Foreland Avenue — East Cliff incinerator works. 2 houses seriously damaged in Foreland Avenue. Casualties nil.

Again the bombs fell wide of their intended target missing the Copt Point guns.

Sunday 6th October. *1030 hrs — HEs — District affected — junction of Black Bull Road & Fernbank Crescent — Folly Road — Rossendale Road — Morrison Road. 7 houses demolished, 22 houses seriously damaged, 216 houses slightly damaged. Casualties 4 female killed, 1 child killed, 11 male injured, 9 female injured, 7 children injured.*

No "Alert" had sounded when a JU88 released its bomb load in the Junction Station area. The result was one of the most severe so far experienced in the town. When the full extent of the damage was realised, Chief Inspector R.J.

Butcher, later the town's ARP Sub-Controller, and who was the senior officer on duty in the Control Room, telephoned Regional HQ at Maidstone, so as to alert more rescue teams. He just could not believe it when his request was refused. On his own initiative he ordered the local sirens to be sounded and mobilised extra rescue parties from outlying districts.

Two streets of small, terraced dwellings, typical of working class districts of so many English towns, were suddenly and most fearfully devastated by just one German bomber whose mission was to bomb the railway and its sidings. Although there were two other raids on this day it was in this particular area that almost all the casualties occurred.

People were buried under the wreckage of their homes when a row of them collapsed like a pack of cards. The ARP teams, firemen and civilians worked frantically to shift the rubble.

Twenty-seven-year-old Mrs Vera Tanner, the wife of a soldier, had been killed outright and her three children, the youngest not yet one year old, were all found beneath the debris after several hours, at what at one time had been 14 Folly Road.

"I saw something which nearly broke my heart," recalled Sid Lester, ". . . I saw two legs sticking out of the rubble. I scraped away and found a girl bent double — backwards — and dead. We left the dead because we could hear noises from others buried alive. There was one child, still in her cot. She was as filthy as a rag doll in a dustbin. But she survived."

Sid Lester had been tearing away at 24 Folly Road, where ten-year-old Dianna Bently was the victim. Her two sisters were found injured. At 12 Folly Road two other victims were discovered, seventeen-year-old Dorothy Bushell and her boy-friend, seventeen-year-old Gerald Prince, the son of the licencee of the Martello Hotel, Dover Road.

At 30 Morrison Road fifty-nine-year-old Mrs Grace Taylor had been killed while her husband was found injured. Their married daughter, twenty-eight-year-old Mrs Freda Cox, was also a fatal casualty.

In every incident there are always those who have remarkable escapes — "There but for the grace of God go I" was a common enough statement heard throughout the war years. Sid Herbert and his wife, licencee of the Swan Inn, Dover Road, escaped with a few injuries when the public house was almost completely wrecked.

1059 hrs — HEs — District affected — Park Farm — Burrow Road — Gladstone Road. 12 houses slightly damaged. Casualties nil.

1529 hrs — HEs — District affected — St Michael's Street — Foreland Avenue. 2 houses partially demolished, 4 houses extensively damaged, 106 houses slightly damaged. Casualties 1 female injured, 1 child injured.

A stick of bombs fell across houses where in one house Mrs Lydia Rogers and Miss Winifred Carr were seriously injured and were taken to hospital. One

In a town where countless incidents in which men and women selflessly risked their lives for others it is all the more difficult to take one as a typical example. But there is one who emulates the spirit of the rest and that is Police Constable William Thomas Elnor Spain, who was awarded the George Medal for his action in attending to a woman pinned under debris at Marine Terrace on 26th August 1940. PC Spain had joined the Folkestone Police in 1913 and retired in 1943.

In nearly every incident there are stories of remarkable escapes and frequently one heard that well-worn cliché "There But For The Grace Of God, Go I". But here at 30 Morrison Road, luck had run out for 59-year-old Grace Taylor and her 28-year-old daughter Freda Cox, when a Junkers 88 bomber attempted to strike at the nearby railway tracks, on 6th October 1940.
(Folkestone Library)

bomb exploded on an Anderson Shelter, uprooting a tree which was blown 150 yards into another street. Rescuers discovered the family were still indoors!

Dr Robert Lindsay, a fifty-year-old Scot, was in his Dover Road Surgery when he heard the bombs fall in the Folly Road area. He recalled: "I knew they were very close but did not think they were more or less just over the road. I reported to my unit — No.2 Casualty Mobile Unit, Salvation Army Hall in Bradstone Road, and was on duty for several hours because it took some time getting the people out who were buried beneath the wreckage of their homes."

Disregarding his own safety and the increased danger of escaping gas, he crawled through a small gap to reach a trapped youth. "When I reached him he was quite hysterical and not at all pleased to see me. Although he told me he did not want a doctor — the morphia quietened him!"

In the house next door children were trapped. Dr Lindsay recalled: "We heard a whimper and thought it was a cat. In fact, it was the whimper of a baby as it turned out. We sawed through some fallen joists to reach the baby and a little girl. The baby was buried for nearly three hours in total darkness before it was finally released. The girl died shortly afterwards but the baby was miraculously uninjured."

Dr Lindsay had spent about one hour under the wreckage with the youth and about an hour and a half with the other children. His fine work, courage and dedication won tremendous admiration from the rescue teams. He had been practising in Folkestone for just over four years and had served in the RAMC in the First World War in both Mesopotamia and France. He was later awarded the George Medal, London Gazette, Friday 17th January 1941.

Tuesday 8th October. *1130 hrs — HEs — District affected — Radnor Park — Stanbury Crescent. 141 houses damaged. Casualties 1 female injured.*

The Primate, speaking at Canterbury Diocesan Conference, said: ". . . the plight of the coastal towns is appalling — the population of Folkestone is down from 47,000 to 11,000 and thousands of houses are empty with whole streets almost entirely deserted and trade has largely vanished."

Even so, while bombs were falling around those Folkestonians who remained, some of them were having an impromptu birthday party in — of all places — an air raid shelter close to Radnor Park. One woman out of a number who regularly used the shelter was tucking into cakes and scones, brought from a nearby home, whilst shrapnel and bomb fragments were flying around the streets. The make-shift table, covered with a damask tablecloth, was adorned with vases of fresh-cut flowers adding a touch of colour to the drab surroundings.

It was shortly after 12 o'clock when Staffel-Kapitan Oberleutnant Werner Voigt got into difficulties when his Messerschmitt Bf109 was damaged by ack-ack. He brought the fighter over the Downs and right over the town, obviously making for the Channel. Anti-aircraft gunners had been on "stand-to" since early morning. The sky became pock-marked with black smudges as shells burst around Voigt's already damaged aircraft. Voigt was the recipient, even at this early stage of the war, of the Iron Cross First and Second Class. He suddenly felt his aircraft lurch as if pushed to one side by an unseen hand. He released his cockpit hood as his machine veered towards the Warren where it hopped and skipped from wave top to wave top like a flat stone skimmed across an expanse of still water.

Voigt's ignominious arrival at the seashore delighted the troops camped beneath the cliff. They ran down the steep paths to stand at the water's edge in chest-heaving triumph. The luckless pilot was taken to Folkestone Police Station by Inspector Floyd and PC Williams.

Thursday 10th October. *1538 hrs — HEs — District affected — East Cliff. Damage nil. Casualties nil.*

Jettisoned bombs fell on open ground. No one saw the aircraft responsible.

Mentioned in an official report as "working-class dwellings", these traditional terraced houses in Grove Road were no match for the blast effects of 500 kilo bombs released by Messerschmitt fighter-bombers in October 1940. (Folkestone Library)

Miss Irene Briscoe took the lead in Don Sesta's orchestra at Bobby's Restaurant. She had previously toured the country with the Ladies' Saxtette. Bobby's was then featuring tea dances on Saturday and Wednesday afternoons. A large notice was prominently displayed in the window:

"In accordance with the expressed desire of the Government that business should proceed as normally as is reasonably possible during air raid warnings, Bobby's have decided to keep open during warnings and give a second interval warning when danger appears imminent. A large shelter, which has been considerably strengthened, is available for patrons in emergencies."

Friday 11th October. 1100 hrs — HEs — District affected — The Riveria, Sandgate. 50 yards of sea wall demolished, 4 houses seriously damaged, 37 houses slightly damaged. Casualties nil.

The Luftwaffe had sustained severe losses during the last six weeks and were now using bomb-carrying Messerschmitt Bf109 fighters. These raids were dubbed "Tip-and-run" raids and were to bring a new kind of terror to coastal towns, for invariably the low-flying fighter-bombers reached our coast unobserved by radar. Folkestone was quite unprepared for this new mode of attack, the first the town knew of it was when half of the Sandgate sea wall was demolished and the German aircraft were already returning to their bases in France when the "Alert" was sounded.

66

1203 hrs — HEs — District affected — Grove Road — Julian Road — Wilton Road. 36 houses seriously damaged, 193 houses slightly damaged. Casualties 1 male killed, 2 male injured, 6 female injured, 2 children injured.

The second attack took place an hour later when several people were injured, some seriously. One of those taken to hospital seriously injured later died. He was eighteen-year-old Arthur Foreman of 68 Grove Road, where his fourteen-year-old sister Beryl was also injured. Others injured were Mrs Ethel Cronin and her baby daughter, and Mrs Harriett McCrow. Houses, shops, a garage and Mundella School, now used as an ARP first aid post, were seriously damaged by blast.

Mrs J. Foreman, an East Kent bus conductress, had a most frightening experience: "When my children were taken to Wales we decided we would get a smaller house. There were plenty at the time and we managed to find one in Grove Road. We were in it just three weeks when a bomb fell in the road and fractured a gas main. As we had only been there a short time we didn't know who the other tenants were. But someone knew I was in the house alone when it was demolished. I could hear a baby crying and found a little girl, but the mother was pinned down. I ran with the baby to what was then the Railway Tavern Inn. I also saw a mother looking for her son. I'm glad I found him before she did. I covered him up with my coat."

"After leaving the baby in the pub, I heard someone say that a Mr Jack Foreman (the name of my husband), had been killed. Imagine my horror when I heard! I asked who was lying beneath the sheet. They confirmed the name but would not let me see him. So I snatched the sheet away. 'Good God!', I said, 'you have the wrong man. That's not my husband!' The mother came up and just said 'Poor Jackie'. When I asked her what her name was she replied 'Foreman'. I don't think anyone could have believed it, but it was so. We only lived four doors away from each other!"

1245 hrs — HEs — District affected — Sidney Street — Alder Road — Golf Links. 8 houses seriously damaged, 84 houses slightly damaged. Casualties nil.

There was still enough good weather in October to help Hitler's invasion prospects, if he had so wished. But Marshal Goering was finding it more convenient to use new tactics to demoralize the British. The third wave of fighter-bombers had arrived near Seabrook and raced over Sandgate and on to Folkestone before anyone knew they were there. They suddenly changed course, avoiding the Downs, and dropped their bombs one after the other. After the long, glorious summer, during which both sides had been engaged in almost continuous air fighting, pilots were feeling the strain. But Goering's new tactics placed an even greater strain not only on the pilots, but also on the civilian population. Townspeople were accepting air raids as part of everyday life and were, more than ever, feeling a touch of pride in finding themselves well and truly in the "front line".

The night of 18th November 1940 saw the heaviest casualties in the town when a parachute mine exploded on Beach Street, shortly after 4.00 am. In all, fourteen people were killed and sixty injured. Fifty-six shops and houses were either demolished or partially demolished and more than 800 damaged, with a further 700 seriously affected. So widespread was the damage that much of the area was never rebuilt.

Tuesday 15th October. *1130 hrs — HEs — District affected — Gas Works Allotments, Archer Road. 1 house seriously damaged, 56 houses slightly damaged. Casualties nil.*

No further information available.

1611 hrs — HEs — District affected — Dawson Road — Radnor Park Road West. 3 houses demolished, 12 houses seriously damaged, 35 houses slightly damaged. Casualties 3 female injured.

Both attacks were made by Messerschmitt fighter-bombers. No further information available.

Thursday 17th October. *1634 hrs — HEs — District affected — junction of Dover Road and Alexandra Street. 1 public house seriously damaged, 5 houses seriously damaged, 14 houses slightly damaged. Casualties nil.*

Fighter-bombers again made their attack at low-level, slipping in at almost sea-level before the Observer Post personnel could spot them. Then it was too late. The maze of track, storage buildings and wagons at the Junction Station was the target. The Railway Bell public house received a direct hit which demolished part of the structure blocking the main Dover Road with rubble. When the rescue teams arrived it was feared there may have been people inside. Fortunately Mr G. Gumbrell, the licencee, his wife and daughter were watching

Ann Sheridan and Humphrey Bogart in "It All Came True" showing at the Central Cinema. Their home had been wrecked just a short time before they left the cinema.

Friday 18th October. *1506 hrs — "E.E. Gee" fires a shell.*

Naval observation posts along the coast between Dover and Folkestone spotted a flotilla of German E-Boats heading towards Dungeness at 24,000 yards range. The 9.2-inch gun named "E.E. Gee" was already in position near the Warren Halt sidings when "Action Stations" was given. The huge barrel swung round at right angles to the track upon which the steel carriage rested. A shell and charge was loaded into the breech. Round One was fired and was observed to fall beyond the flotilla. Immediately the E-Boats altered course towards France and were soon out of range. Unable to cope with the sideways thrust of the recoil action, "E.E. Gee" jumped off the rails! It took twelve hours to get the 86-ton bogie back on an even keel.

Sunday 20th October. *1423 hrs — HEs — District affected — Sports Ground, Cheriton. Damage nil. Casualties nil.*

No further information available.

Tuesday 22nd October. *1152 hrs — HEs — District affected — Warren Road. 5 houses demolished, 25 houses damaged. Casualties 2 male injured, 1 female injured.*

The Observer Post at Abbotts Cliff plotted a small formation of bomb-carrying Messerschmitts heading towards the coast at low-level. While the handle of the field telephone was being furiously turned, the formation split into single attacking aircraft, each veering off in a different direction. Just one 500-kilo high-explosive bomb wrecked five houses in Warren Road — Nos 15 to 23.

1330 to 1336 hrs — HEs & oil-incendiary — District affected — Shakespeare Terrace — Clifton Gardens — Folkestone Harbour — Marine Parade — Coast-guard Cottages. 2 houses demolished, 20 houses damaged, extensive damage to interior of Martin Walter's showrooms. Casualties nil.

Documents fail to identify the type of aircraft used which released four high-explosive bombs in the early afternoon. One of them was an oil-incendiary type which struck the side of Martin Walter's showroom at the corner of Sandgate Road and Shakespeare Terrace. It fell down a vehicle lift shaft and exploded in the basement, causing considerable damage and demolishing a couple of houses.

1620 hrs — HEs — District affected — Foreland Avenue allotments — Grimston Gardens playing fields. 6 houses slightly damaged.

Although this was another fighter-bomber attack, no further information is available.

Set to detonate before hitting the ground, the second of two parachute mines exploded above Rossendale Road on the night of 18th November 1940. Dwellings were flattened like paper and the area became, in seconds, a moonscape of wreckage. Rescuers worked feverishly for hours beneath the macabre glow of arc-lamps to reach those who were trapped.

Saturday 26th October. *1655 hrs — HEs — District affected — Bouverie Road West — Castle Hill Avenue — Marine Parade — Shorncliffe Camp (RASC Lines) — Parish Churchyard. 1 house demolished, 1 house partially demolished, 8 houses seriously damaged, 11 houses slightly damaged. Casualties 1 female killed, 3 male injured.*

Four Messerschmitt fighter-bombers spread over the town at almost roof-top level. One bomb exploded in the Parish Church area which seriously damaged the council offices on the Bayle. A chimney collapsed through the roof of one office where Charles Holden was injured, and the major's house was seriously damaged by blast and flying masonry. Hundreds of stained-glass windowpanes cracked in the nearby church.

Another bomb made a direct hit on 24 Castle Hill Avenue, where Mrs Louisa Marion Fitzgerald died instantly. Her husband, Dr Edward Desmond Fitzgerald, was seriously injured and died of his wounds the next day at Victoria Hospital. Several people living in upper-floor flats were stranded and could only be rescued by the fire escape ladders.

Sunday 27th October. *0735 hrs — HEs — District affected — Wear Bay Road. 7 houses seriously damaged, 32 houses slightly damaged. Casualties nil.*

This "Tip-and-run" raid very nearly hit the gun battery.

Monday 28th October. *0650 hrs — HEs — District affected — King's Road — St Martin's Road — Whitby Road. 5 houses slightly damaged. Casualties nil.*
Another "Tip-and-run" raid by fighter-bombers.

1000 hrs — HEs — District affected — Menage (Shorncliffe Camp) water main to garrison fractured. Casualties nil.
A single fighter-bomber attack.

Wednesday 30th October. *1605 hrs — HEs — District affected — Grove Road (railway embankment). 1 house demolished, 10 houses seriously damaged, 25 houses slightly damaged. Casualties nil.*
A swift fighter-bomber raid demolished houses at the junction of Grove Road and Abbott Road — Nos 10 and 12.

Saturday 2nd November. *A letter to 'Folkestone & Hythe District Herald'.*
"Sir,

"Could not the 'Spotter' system, advocated for the large industrial concern, be adopted for all public warnings? These 'Tip-and-run' raids dislocate trade and waste much time. We were first told that it was a public duty to take shelter. Because of the interruption to our war effort in the production of munitions, we were next told that work should go on until a 'Danger Imminent' warning is given.

"How can small traders continue working after the 'Alert' or ask their staff, including young people, to do so, or for that matter, expect their customers to call unless they are to be warned when danger is near?

"Those who, like myself and staff, have endeavoured to carry on after the 'Alert', have been close to death and destruction. The present haphazard method results in much loss of what little trade is left to traders in coast towns; and this, too, interrupts our war effort, for we are prevented from earning sufficient to save enough to 'Lend to Defend'.

"Anything the Government could do to help traders to get their work done during raids and to encourage evacuees to return to their home towns now that invasion dangers are receding, or anything Mr Churchill could do to implement his promise to consider the revision of the warning methods and to abolish the 'Banshee Wailings', should be done quickly if the maximum revenue from the trading community in these areas is needed for the National effort."

Signed: War-wrecked Trader.
Coal shortage in Folkestone — each householder was to be rationed to 5 cwt (hundredweight) of coal per month.

Monday 4th November. *1755 hrs — Machine-gunning — District affected — Cheriton High Street. Damage slight. Casualties 2 slightly injured.*
A Heinkel 111 bomber was crossing the coast on its way to France. It was very low and eyewitnesses recall it had been hit by AA fire. As it flew over Cheriton

The destructive power of a parachute mine is total. Above: another view of Rossendale Road which took the full force of the explosion instead of the Junction Station and its maze of railway tracks just two hundred yards away.

High Street the gunners sprayed the streets with bullets. People ran for shelter as bullets whizzed around them indiscriminately. A husband and wife were sitting beside their dining room window when the glass shattered. They both received cuts. Perhaps the most bizarre incident involved a van driver who was making a late delivery to a grocer's shop. Three tins of salmon were pierced by bullets as he carried them across the pavement. Needless to say he dropped the salmon and dived beneath his van.

Tuesday 5th November. *0315 hrs — HEs — District affected — Dallas Brett Crescent. 15 houses slightly damaged. Casualties nil.*

Eight 250-kilo bombs were thought to have been released by a German bomber returning to France. Bombs fell on open land near the brickworks.

1130 hrs — HEs — District affected — Hospital Hill near Sandgate Esplanade. Military fumigating station damaged — public shelter, battery points, windows broken. Casualties 1 male soldier killed.

For the second year Guy Fawkes was forgotten and the day passed without fireworks or bonfires, although a local journalist wrote: "Maybe the fireworks we see daily are sufficient to satisfy us."

ARP wardens and members of the voluntary fire-fighting parties, recognised by local authorities, have been given the same right of entry powers for fire-fighting purposes as regular firemen and members of the AFS.

Alderman George A. Gurr was elected Mayor of Folkestone for another year, his third year of office. It was to be his last.

Saturday 9th November. 1238 hrs — HEs — District affected — junction of Cheriton Road and Marler Road — Broomfield Road — Park Farm Brickfields. 5 houses partially demolished, 3 houses seriously damaged, 7 houses slightly damaged. Casualties nil.

Eyewitnesses saw a single JU88 bomber alter course when ack-ack shells, fired from the 3-inch battery on the Downs, got too close for comfort. The bomber released his load of 250-kilo bombs which straddled the area from the brickfields to Cheriton High Street.

Monday 11th November (Armistice Day). 1310 hrs — HEs — District affected — the Stade — Tram Road — railway bank near Darlington Arch — Julian Road (32). 2 premises demolished, 2 houses partly demolished, 24 houses seriously damaged, 262 houses slightly damaged. Casualties 8 male injured, 3 female injured, 2 children injured.

As early as 0600 hrs enemy fighter-bomber sweeps had been operating over the south east. A little later bomber groups were heading for various targets inland.

Sea mists had just cleared away when two groups of Messerschmitt fighter-bombers suddenly appeared, unannounced, over the harbour and released their bombs almost at once. One bomb exploded on the Fisherman's Bethel beside the railway arch on the Stade. It was here that Skipper Oldman, his wife and daughter Violet were trapped in the wreckage. Several occupants were crawling under the billiard table when the walls caved in and were thankful for the gift of the table from Sir Philip Sassoon the year before. But despite the table's protection five occupants were seriously injured and were taken to hospital. Other property damaged included the workshops of J. Ovenden & Sons, Tolputt's Timber Yard, the Pavilion Shades public house and Peden's Stables, used for many years in connection with the transport of some of the world's most famous racehorses across the Channel. When the bomb exploded, the stables, on the corner of Tram Road and South Street, were fortunately unoccupied.

Wednesday 13th November. 1355 hrs — HEs — District affected — Sidney Street (George Spurgeon School) — Bradley Road (Co-op Bakery) — Denmark Street — Warren Way. School and bakery partly demolished, 20 houses seriously damaged, 103 houses slightly damaged. Casualties 1 male killed, 2 female injured.

Several enemy bomber formations had passed over the town just before mid-day. But this particular attack was made by fighter-bombers. The George

73

By January 1941, "D" Company, 8th Battalion Home Guard (Folkestone), drawn from the town's Gas Company, had been supplied with greatcoats. Precious little equipment had arrived though and they were still performing sentry duties within the gasworks compound at night with only a pick-axe handle. Eventually, however, each man was issued with a rifle and the gasworks unit would be out on Hythe ranges on Sundays, or practising on machine-guns at the brickfields below Caesar's Camp.   (Sidney Lester)

Spurgeon School, evacuated and used by the ARP as a depot, was the first hit and where thirty-two-year-old William Baker, an ARP member, was killed. The Co-operative bakery in Bradley Road was almost destroyed.

Monday 18th November. *0420 hrs — HEs (parachute mines) — District affected — Beach Street — junction of Folly Road and Rossendale Road. 56 houses and buildings demolished or partly demolished, 674 houses seriously damaged, 215 houses slightly damaged. Casualties 8 male killed, 6 female killed, 20 male injured, 35 female injured, 5 children injured.*

It was a bright, moonlit night and stars glistened in the sky like diamonds. There was a keen sea breeze which rustled the brown, crisp leaves which had yet to fall from the trees, a breeze which disturbed the odd paper bag in the gutter. Herring Gulls preened their feathers between the chimney-pots. Police Constable Spain hung the telephone receiver back on its hook then closed and locked the door of the little blue box.

Within just a few seconds this tranquil scene was to erupt into a hideous nightmare, when a large number of sleeping people were suddenly buried under the wreckage of their homes and shops. Set to detonate before hitting the ground two large parachute mines exploded within yards of their target just after 4 am.

The blast of the first to explode above Rossendale Road and Folly Road flattened dwellings like paper and caused widespread damage. Some had remarkable escapes and were either rescued alive or managed to crawl out from

74

beneath the debris unassisted. Others were found dead several hours later in the macabre glow of arc-lamps. Rescue teams were assisted by members of the Pioneer Corps.

In the congested Beach Street area near the harbour, several public houses were wiped out, little cafés and restaurants had gone and a baker's shop was just a heap of rubble. It was from this pile of broken masonry, rafters and joists, that by a miracle the injured baker and his wife escaped with their lives.

Part of the Royal George Hotel collapsed into the road, its gaunt walls cracked and scarred, bare rooms which had shed their furniture into the basement were now open to public scrutiny. In one room, several floors up, there hung a brass bedstead, balanced precariously over the edge of shattered floor-boards.

Members of the rescue teams looked up at the torn wallpaper which hung in shreds. A picture frame, tilted at right-angles, clung to a chimney-breast which showed signs of collapse. The body of an hotel employee was known to be in the building but for some time it was left there, impossible to reach for fear of the building coming down on the rescuers.

While the teams moved tons of rubble in their frantic search for victims, the proprietors of a little tea shop, the premises twisted beyond recognition, served gallons of hot tea.

As some of the bodies were recovered their identity for a time was unknown. Four were women, three were wearing a wedding ring and the fourth an engagement ring. There were no other means of identification.

PC Spain, who had recently been awarded the George Medal for bravery during another air raid, actually saw the raider in the moonlight. He was later concussed by the terrific explosion.

"It was not more than about 800 feet up when I saw it bank," Spain recalled later, "almost immediately there was a terrific explosion and flash. Something seemed to give me a fearful blow in the chest. I was knocked out completely. When I came round I was on the ground in the entrance to a pub! I heard voices inside and on entering found three people trapped at the foot of the staircase. I picked up a little girl and brought her out. I carried her away from the scene of devastation but, on my way to the police station, I collapsed."

Sixty-eight-year-old Charles Colegate was trapped under rubble which had been 16 Beach Street for eleven hours before they reached him. He died in hospital the next day. His wife Sophia was already dead, along with Gladys Aino, who also lived at the same address. At 11 Beach Street, Rose and Charles Rainsford had been killed, also Walter Tame, but they never found Mrs Tame. In the South Foreland Hotel cellar they found twenty-year-old Ronald Early; from what was left of 14 Beach Street they found George Saunders; they later recovered Charles Stubbington from the Royal George Hotel. William Maskell, the 71-year-old licencee of the Wonder Tavern, a well-known personality in the nearby fishmarket, had also been killed.

Townspeople were stunned at first by this type of indiscriminate, 'senseless destruction of civilian property, not to mention lives. But in the cold light of day

The Mayor, Alderman George A. Gurr, had said during a council debate on whether to supply beds for people using air raid shelters: ". . . the council were considering arrangements to put up 1,000 beds or bunks and possibly one of the large hotels would be used. Personally . . ." he went on, and now in his third year of office, ". . . I think it best to stay home in bed!" The parachute mine, which drifted slowly on to Morehall Avenue in the early hours of 29th May 1941, caused thirteen fatalities out of a total of 56 casualties, the Mayor and his wife among them. Over 600 dwellings were damaged. (Folkestone Library)

it was soon realised the German bomber crew had been aiming at the railway line which ran from the Junction Station to the harbour.

The spirit of the people in that kind of horror and devastation was reflected in the words of one housewife who, after her home had been levelled to the ground at Rossendale Road, said to Lord Knolly's, the Deputy Regional Commissioner, who visited the town just a few hours later, "I had a wonderful stroke of luck this afternoon — I found my three Christmas puddings!"

By noon, two fish-hawkers had retrieved their barrows from under the debris and were selling herrings.

Tuesday 3rd December. *Incident — fishermen shot by sentry.*

It had been the legitimate boast of the Folkestone fishermen that not even Hitler, nor his impending invasion, could stop them fishing. They regarded the barbed-wire and concrete block defences with contempt and had little regard for the sentries who operated the boom-barricade. As for the latter, they were hardly expected to understand the professionalism of the fishing fraternity and in fact, there was no compensating advantage for them to even begin to comprehend the variations in tides.

76

On the other hand, the fishermen, whose fishing grounds were seriously reduced by Royal Navy minefields, knew only too well the advantages of laying their long-lines between the Southern Railway Pier head and the sad-looking Victoria Pier. The intricacy of long-lining was child's play to Percy Bricknell, who was "hell-bent" on getting his lines out before darkness curtailed their activities. FE26 moved out slowly in reverse until her bow was clear of other boats quietly riding their moorings in the harbour. On the quayside above the boom-barricade stood a sentry in conversation with a local coastguard. At the tiller Ted Fagg eased FE26 towards the harbour entrance and waited for the boom to be lowered. But nothing happened. Tiller hard over FE26 went round in a complete circle to make another approach. There was an exchange of words between the sentry, Percy, Ted and John Brazier, the gist of which has long been forgotten in the passage of time. Doubtless the exchange of words became heated while FE26 went round in circles.

Going round for the umpteenth time Percy, standing in the bow, was astonished to see the sentry raise his rifle. The moment of revelation came when Ted Fagg felt a bullet go through his hand. The same bullet went through Brazier's sou'wester and struck Percy in the left thigh.

While a fresh-faced lieutenant bandaged Percy's bleeding wound at the quayside, the sentry was being double-marched into close arrest. The sentry was later court-martialed.

Thursday 12th December. *1159 hrs — HEs — District affected — East Cliff Bathing Establishments damaged. Casualties nil.*

This was the last high explosive bomb to fall on Folkestone in 1940, and was released by a bomber returning to its French base.

The Archbishop of Canterbury made an attempt to obtain some relaxation of the Government's order prohibiting the ringing of church bells. His Grace wrote in the 'Canterbury Diocesan Gazette', "I have made every effort to persuade the Government to amend the existing order and to permit the bells to be rung on Sundays only for a short time before the hours appointed in each place for Divine Service. I am very sorry to say that in spite of all my efforts which were most sympathetically received, the Secretary of State for War has informed me that the military authorities are unable to advise any change in the existing order and that he feels bound to accept their decision. This will give real disappointment in all parts of the country. The sound of the church bells after long silence would have done much to cheer our people at a time of great strain. It would have been a fitting reminder at this solemn time of the duty of the public acknowledgement of GOD."

It was little consolation to bereaved families to be told that Folkestonians stood up to nothing like the traumatic carnage that consumed large cities. There were, after all, in this comparatively quiet seaside resort, nearly 1,000 casualties. Above: members of the Mundella School ARP First Aid Team in 1941.

The pride of the Borough of Folkestone Fire Brigade, the 1938 Merryweather Turntable Escape Ladder. Its 100 feet steel ladder was invaluable during the war years. This photograph was taken in 1944, at the side of the Maltby's Showrooms in Shakespeare Terrace. Features of interest are the white lines painted on the bumper and round the mudguards and the headlight masks. EKP 395 was still in use in 1957.

1941

Headline in 'Folkestone Herald' for January 4th 1941:
ARMY OF FIRE SPOTTERS
PERIL OF RAIDERS' INCENDIARIES
APPEAL TO ALL FOLKESTONE RESIDENTS
ENROL AT NEAREST WARDEN'S POST NOW!

It is the duty of every man in Folkestone to enrol as a fire spotter. The Ministry of Home Security has issued an appeal to all to help in the work of defeating incendiary bombs dropped by raiders.

In Folkestone the Chief Constable, who is ARP Controller, and the Chief Air Raid Warden, have devised a scheme of fire spotting that will cover the whole town. The success of the scheme is dependent upon a ready response from men and women who will give their services as spotters.

Every householder is asked to protect his or her property from the effects of incendiary bombs. Prompt action if fire bombs are dropped by raiders can prevent fires and nullify any attempts to set the town on fire. The scheme for spotting and fire-fighting fire bombs is as follows:

1. Each warden's sector will be divided into groups of 12 to 20 buildings.
2. Each occupied house to be called upon to provide at least one person for duty as fire spotter during periods of 'Alert'.
3. As far as possible a stirrup pump will be allocated to each group and a party of spotters trained and organised to operate same.
4. Stirrup pumps issued to individuals must always be available.
5. Sandbags, half-filled, will be placed at a convenient site in each group area for smothering bombs.
6. Every householder should keep a bucket of water filled outside his front door where this will not cause obstruction to the public.
7. In houses and premises left unoccupied at night the raising of blinds or removal of other black-out protection in upper floors should be carried out. If such houses and properties are locked up the keys should be left with a member of the group area fire party or in some place where they are immediately and readily accessible.

The Chief Air Raid Warden issues the following appeal to the people of Folkestone:

In view of the lines upon which air warfare is developing it is imperative that additional precautions, as outlined by the Home Secretary in his recent broadcast, be taken to prevent the spread of fire from incendiary bombs.

It is your duty to assist in this work by enrolling at once at the nearest Warden's Post as a fire spotter.

"The Navy's Here"

FOLKESTONE
WARSHIP
WEEK

March 21st to 28th, 1942.

PROGRAMME - - 6d.

Including

FREE ADMISSION to the EXHIBITION

Our Aim: £136,500 to "adopt" H.M.S. Folkestone.

FOLKESTONE AND DISTRICT

SALUTE the SOLDIER
WEEK April 22—29

Remember — It may be *your* house on which incendiary bombs fall! Why depend on other people to protect *your* property and do *your* work!

In helping yourself you are helping others to preserve your own and others' property.

For further particulars consult your air raid warden."

Tuesday 7th January. *1415 hrs* — *HEs* — *District affected* — *Dover Road near Junction Station. 4 houses partly demolished, 11 houses seriously damaged, 61 houses slightly damaged. Casualties 1 female killed, 1 female slightly injured.*

A lone Heinkel bomber released a stick of six bombs near the entrance to the Junction Station. They fell behind Nos 198, 200, 202 and 204 Dover Road. It was in the latter that Mrs Charlotte Taylor, a 72-year-old widow, who was upstairs at the time, was fatally injured when the roof caved in. Her daughter, Grace Taylor, who was downstairs, escaped with cuts and bruises. The Heinkel turned towards the sea and machine-gunned Tontine Street where people shopping scattered to escape bullets. One man crawled beneath a stationary car, the roof of which received several bullet holes.

Friday 17th January. *0105 hrs — HEs — District affected — Burrow Road. 4 houses demolished, 8 houses partly demolished, 25 houses seriously damaged, 75 houses slightly damaged. Casualties 4 male injured, 2 female injured, 1 child injured.*

A heavy bomb, probably a 1,000-kilo, demolished Nos 31 to 37 Burrow Road in the early hours of the morning and, although no one was killed, there was extensive damage, rendering many families homeless.

In response to the fire spotters' appeal over 3,200 people came forward as volunteers. In the first week over 15,000 sandbags had been placed at strategic points in the streets at about 25-yard intervals.

Monday 27th January. *1450 hrs — Shelling — District affected — Wellington Road, Cheriton. Damage nil. Casualties nil.*

Tuesday 28th January. *1740 hrs — Machine-gun fire — District affected — Sandgate.*

The "Kent War Diaries" record, "Sandgate — Sentry on duty observed two enemy motor torpedo boats about 200 yards off shore. Boats fired two bursts of machine-gun fire. (Unconfirmed)"

Perhaps the only confirmation we have is that recalled by Eric Hart of the Home Guard unit at Sandgate Castle: "Although not on duty at the time, I heard about an incident at the castle when the powerful 'surflight' was switched on accidentally, and its beam seaward silhouetted some of our motor torpedo boats, who at the time were tangling with German E-boats. I understand that a frenzied phone call had the castle field-phone jumping off its mounting on the wall before it was switched off!"

Sunday 2nd February. *1556 hrs — HEs — District affected — Cheriton High Street — Cobden Road — Risborough Lane — Page's Lane. 1 house demolished, 2 store-sheds demolished, 2 houses partly demolished, 12 houses slightly damaged. Casualties 1 male injured, 2 female injured.*

A JU88 dropped a stick of bombs in the Cheriton area just before 4 pm. All the bombs fell in a populated area where one house, No.137 Cheriton High Street, was completely demolished. Fortunately all the family were out; Percy Ames was at work and his wife and daughter were at All Souls' Church, not more than 150 yards away from their home. When the rescue teams arrived they feared the occupants were buried beneath the rubble but, despite the damage caused by the high explosive bomb, the family dog was rescued alive.

Two other bombs fell near Cheriton Hall Station near the yard of S.H. Page & Sons, builders in Risborough Lane, where a car was wrecked in a shed. Six bombs were dropped, two more falling in Cobden Road where lock-up sheds were wrecked. A gas main was fractured causing traffic diversions on the A20.

Saturday 8th February. *1530 hrs — Machine-gunning — District affected — Cheriton and Morehall. Casualties nil.*

Two Messerschmitt fighters opened fire upon shoppers in the late afternoon. Footballers at Morehall fell on their faces when cannon-shells and bullets ripped into the turf. Mr and Mrs J. Stewart of 61 Morehall Avenue, had a narrow escape when a cannon-shell penetrated their roof, went through a bedroom ceiling then out through a window. They were both downstairs at the time.

A cheque for £5,000, dated 5th February 1941, was sent to Lord Beaverbrook by the 'Folkestone & Hythe District Herald', to buy a Spitfire.

New Defence Regulations

Instances have occurred in which enemy airmen who have landed in this country have given to civilians as "souvenirs" a flying helmet or other parts of their equipment. Articles such as goggles, field boots, diaries etc, which may seem to be trivial may yet offer valuable information to the military authorities. The Defence Regulations made it an offence to retain any such article.

In view of the urgent need for paper economy telephone directories were suspended.

Monday 17th February. *0010 hrs — Parachute mine — District affected — the beach at Parade, Sandgate. 40 houses seriously damaged, 81 houses damaged. Casualties nil.*

Tuesday 25th February. *2300 hrs — HEs & IBs — District affected — Allendale Road — Joyes Road — Varne Road — Varne Place — Bradstone Avenue — Blackbull Road — Folly Road — Grove Road — Dover Road. 11 houses slightly damaged, 2 houses partially demolished, crater in road, water and gas mains fractured, 1 depository completely burnt out, 1 depository top floor only burnt out. Casualties nil.*

When a shower of incendiaries was dropped around the Junction area late on Tuesday night a number of fires broke out and were extinguished rather more quickly than had at first been anticipated. Many of the incendiaries were dealt with by placing sandbags over them, especially those which had fallen in street areas. Others which had fallen on buildings were tackled by the newly formed fire teams and in less than half an hour of their arrival the fires were more or less put out. The exception, however, was a more serious blaze at Messrs Thompson's furniture store and depository in Grove Road. Flames leapt up from the building while sparks flew on the night breeze. The concentration of fire services brought the fire under control within half an hour although the building was burned to the ground. Another Thompson store at No.139 Dover Road was also set ablaze when incendiaries penetrated the roof. The top floor was gutted but the remainder of the building was only affected by thousands of gallons of water, which ran down the roads like a river in full flood.

Pockets of fire were started in several places but the fire teams dealt with them with sandbags and stirrup pumps. The high explosive bombs fell mostly in Varne Road and Varne Place, No11 Varne Road receiving a direct hit while another bomb caused a huge crater to appear in Varne Place.

There is an unexpected sequel to the night's events recalled by Section Officer R.R. Fry, a member of the Folkestone Auxiliary Fire Service, who wrote thirty-three years later: "Off duty one evening I was travelling on a bus to Wood Avenue. As we turned into Canterbury Road, flares burst in the sky above us, bathing the town in soft orange light. They swung slowly, suspended on parachutes, while the noise of circling aircraft could be heard. No sirens sounded, no searchlights or guns opened up. An ominous silence prevailed. I ran a few yards along Joyes Road to warn my father that something peculiar was about to happen, and returned to Canterbury Road in time to catch the bus on its return journey. As we reached the junction of Canterbury Road and Dover Road, incendiaries fell all around us. They struck roofs and disappeared inside with a flash. They stuck in pavements and in the road and wherever they hit they started to burn. The orange light of the flares was lost in the bright incandescence of burning magnesium.

"The bus driver pulled under the railway arch and stopped. 'I can't go down there through that lot,' he said. 'Don't you know bombs will follow? Incendiaries are only dropped to mark a target,' I told him. The driver replied: 'I never thought of that' and moved the bus carefully down the blazing roadway. Behind us we felt the thud of falling bombs. At the top of Tontine Street he checked to let me off calling 'Good Luck!' as I ran across to the fire station. The entrance was crowded with men staring at the tremendous glow growing in the direction of Dover. Someone said: 'Dover ain't half copped it.' I replied: 'Not Dover — Dover Road!'.

"As I ran to the watch room, sirens sounded belatedly. Available crews left quickly. I took a light pump and headed for the scene. Dover Road was alight on both sides. Thompson's furniture depositories in Dover Road and Grove Road were both burning. Houses were alight in Grove Road and also in the already badly damaged Rossendale Road and Folly Road. Our light pump was not of much use on the larger fires, but in Rossendale Road, a huge pile of salvaged timber burnt like a monstrous November 5th bonfire. We took this on.

"Pumps were constantly arriving from various posts around the town, but there were plenty of fires too.

"Thompson's Grove Road depository was tackled by two crews working into the building from opposite ends. Some of the old rivalry between regulars and auxiliaries still lingered. Bob Green, handling a line from a brigade machine, caught sight of auxiliaries moving in through stacks of furniture, similarly employed. A quick flick with the hose, followed by indignant yells, indicated his aim was good. 'You're not a fireman until you're wet,' shouted Bob. But the auxiliaries were learning fast. The moment for revenge came, and they did not

Junkers JU88 medium bombers often made low-level attacks on Folkestone, carrying 250 kilo or 500 kilo bombs.

The Heinkel 111 bomber usually released its bomb load over the town when on its way back to the French coast. It carried, in addition to 250 and 500 kilo bombs, incendiary canisters.

miss. Two damp crews struggled manfully with a task clearly beyond them. The Grove Road depository burnt down to ground level.

"As we came across incendiaries that had failed to ignite, we found they were not the usual type. These were hexagonal in shape, heavily weighted at one end and had two distinct parts. One, much lighter in material, burst on ignition and showered burning fragments around. They seemed much more formidable than the usual German pattern.

"We were fortunate in one respect. Damage was caused by fire only, and casualties were slight. Bombs had missed the area and we were not called upon to search shattered buildings for casualties. We had gained control by midnight.

"The next morning, all crews who had been engaged were paraded and warned that if members of the press came seeking information, none was to be offered. Anyone who had picked up leaflets during the night was asked to produce them. We had found none but a number of men had.

"Clearly they should have been delivered on the other side of the Channel. They outlined the dire fate awaiting Germans attempting to set foot on British soil, carrying sketches of the sea burning etc.

"It seemed that a Polish crew had flown out over Dungeness, crossed the Hythe Bay and come in over Folkestone, thinking they had reached Boulogne. Their target should have been invasion barges. Security decreed that news of this incident had to be suppressed. Fortunately for Folkestone, the bomb-aimer's skill was no better than that of the navigator's. The bombs fell mainly in the open on Wear Bay, causing little damage."

Saturday 1st March. 0815 hrs — Shell — District affected — Command Gymnasium, Shorncliffe Camp. Gymnasium partly demolished, minor damage to military buildings. Casualties nil.

Thursday 6th March.1515 hrs — HEs — District affected — East Kent Road Car Company's garage, Cheriton. No damage, 1 unexploded bomb. Casualties nil.

The "Alert" had just sounded at 3 pm when a lone Dornier 17 bomber was spotted by an Observer Corps post to the west of the town. The sky was overcast with a few breaks here and there. The Dornier seemed to level off at Sandgate and, as it approached Cheriton, began to fire its machine-guns. Bullets sprayed everywhere but any damage was superficial. A Spitfire of 91 Squadron, based at RAF Hawkinge, had already scrambled to intercept the raider. Sergeant Donald McKay, a veteran of many dog-fights both in France before the evacuation and during the Battle of Britain, was climbing above the town and towards the Channel, when he saw splashes in the sea just outside the harbour. McKay spotted the Dornier through a break in the low cloud. He closed in and fired a couple of bursts. The Dornier spun into the water and sank.

Saturday 8th March. 2215 hrs — HEs & IBs — District affected — Junction Station and sidings — Dover Road — Stanbury Crescent — Pilcher & Chittenden's Nursery. 18 houses slightly damaged, Junction Station roof damaged. Casualties 3 male injured.

In the early evening people stood on the Leas and felt the ground shaking beneath their feet, so terrific was the force of explosions coming from the French coastal posts of Boulogne and Calais. The scene was awe-inspiring and provided excitement, not least because it was the enemy who was now receiving his "just deserts". Hitler's invasion ports were being pounded by Bomber Command. Now and again a bomber was observed caught in the beams of searchlights which flicked this way and that like huge, luminous tentacles. Bursting anti-aircraft shells above the French towns looked like a grand firework display.

When the excitement had died down, people returned to their homes. At 10 pm the "Alert" sounded. Everyone thought a reprisal attack was imminent and naturally scrambled into their shelters. A single enemy bomber flew over

The Dornier Do17Z was a frequent visitor in 1940 and 1941.

the town at a very high altitude. Searchlights scanned the sky and the AA units at Capel opened fire. Two high explosive bombs dropped on open ground, one of them failed to explode. The Junction Station area was covered with incendiaries where small fires were started. Fire-fighting teams soon had them under control.

Monday 10th March. *1844 hrs — HEs — District affected — The Firs, Cheriton — Danton Pinch. Farm house and buildings partially demolished, 11 houses slightly damaged. Casualties nil.*

Only one high explosive bomb fell on this occasion when a high-flying bomber was returning to its French base.

The compulsory evacuation of schoolchildren remaining in Folkestone was strongly supported during a discussion on the problem at a meeting of the Folkestone Town Council on Wednesday 12th March. The number of children affected in Folkestone was stated as approximately 500. One councillor said: "I don't think we can press this matter too strongly as there are 500 children of school age running wild in the town!"

At the Annual Licensing Sessions, held at the town hall on Wednesday the 12th, the Chief Constable, Mr A.S. Beesley, reported that nine public houses had been destroyed or damaged by enemy action and 35 others had been closed owing to lack of business. Mr W.J. Mason, appearing for the Railway Bell, damaged three times by bombs, said the upper part was being pulled down but it was proposed to put a roof over the ground floor. Plans were also presented with regard to the Royal George Hotel, the upper part of which had also been removed.

A letter appearing in the 'Folkestone Herald' said.
"Sir,

"I heard a cheery optimistic remark on Wednesday last that I think is worth recording. I called at a tobacconist's shop in a much bombed area, just as an aeroplane was diving and swooping in a manner that was rather un-nerving to the assistant and some lady customers. The manager looked outside and came back in with the reassuring news: 'It's all right — they're ours!' A genial lady had followed him in and said: 'Ours! of course they're ours, and they will all be ours before very long!'."

Signed. One of the Others

Saturday 15th March. 0250 hrs — HEs — District affected — Sugar Loaf Hill. 25 houses slightly damaged. Casualties nil.

Wednesday 19th March. 0155 hrs — HEs & IBs — District affected — Cheriton High Street — St Martin's Road. 7 houses demolished, 11 houses partly demolished, 42 houses seriously damaged, 97 houses slightly damaged. Casualties 1 female killed, 2 children killed, 3 male injured, 3 female injured, 2 children injured.

It is perhaps one of the tragedies of the Second World War that in just a split second, harmless, innocent people suddenly became victims. I suppose it could be said of any war. Bombs and even shells do not discriminate between the military and the defenceless civilian, and in Folkestone, no less than anywhere else, the ordinary citizen suffered as a result of enemy action. Enemy Action — a well worn cliché which conceals inadequately the misery and distress that is experienced by so many families.

The siren had sounded its "Alert" signal quite late in the evening when formations of enemy bombers had crossed the coast and headed inland. Fire watchers were getting ready to combat any eventuality. Wardens on duty collected at their respective ARP posts. They waited — they played darts and dominoes, card games and billiards. Home Guard sentries patrolled their positions and mused over events which either had happened since the war began, or the possibilities of an appalling tragedy, yet to be experienced.

Searchlights suddenly flicked on. The familiar drone of an enemy aircraft was heard to the north of the town. Sentries guessed it was an enemy bomber with engine trouble trying to reach the comparative safety of the English Channel.

Then there was that ear-splitting roar of falling bombs.

Mr and Mrs Kimber, a young married couple, were taking their turn at fire watching and were both downstairs when a bomb struck. It was so fortunate for them that they were downstairs. Just a few minutes before they would have been asleep in their bedroom and would most assuredly have been killed. Their bedroom had been crushed beneath the roof slates, and the heavy water tank. At 187 Cheriton High Street, Mrs E.A. Turner was sleeping downstairs with her two daughters aged three and four. A bomb exploded right outside their room. From under plaster, bricks, window frames and glass Mrs Turner found her two

The Junkers JU87 "Stuka" dive-bomber was used against Hawkinge aerodrome in 1940, and also many Channel convoys.

girls and carried them out of the wrecked house. Mr Ernest J.D. Wakefield, a lorry driver, and Mr F.H. Cossum, an ARP warden, were quickly on the scene and both began to search among the debris.

They were searching No.178 Cheriton High Street, when they heard a woman crying for help. While Cossum crawled through a gap in one direction Ernie Wakefield climbed through another gap between collapsed rafters. A baby was crying. They moved bricks and broken furniture. Water cascaded from split pipes and there was the familiar smell of gas escaping from a fractured main. Mr and Mrs Mellow were found injured. Then they came across the child's cot which had been turned over on its side. Heavy rafters were resting on it. The seven-week-old baby was lifted to safety without disturbing the collapsed roof. The baby stopped crying immediately.

In the adjoining house, No.176, death had come suddenly and swiftly. Mrs Alice Griffin, the 29-year-old wife of a soldier, and her two sons, one aged four, the other only eighteen months, were crushed beneath the fallen masonry. Corporal Griffin, the husband, was sleeping in another room and escaped serious injury.

Ernest Wakefield looked at the wreckage of walls and ceilings, the heaps of bricks and rubble, the only visible signs of a home blasted beyond recognition. As he sipped a mug of hot tea at first light, he thought of the other wreckage that cannot be seen, the intimate turmoil of home life between parents and children. There was, he thought, nothing to replace that shattered home.

Friday 21st March. 0743 hrs — HEs — District affected — Park Farm (open ground) — Downs Road. 28 houses slightly damaged. Casualties 2 male injured.

Wednesday 26th March. *1200 hrs — Machine-gunning — District affected — Cheriton and Morehall. Casualties nil.*

Thursday 27th March. *0920 hrs — HEs — District affected — Folkestone Harbour — East Cliff Gardens — East Street — St Andrew's Home. 1 house demolished, 2 houses partly demolished, 3 houses seriously damaged, 131 houses slightly damaged. Casualties 1 male injured.*

Messerschmitt fighter-bombers made a lightning attack in the harbour area. Mrs E. Dalby, a 64-year-old widow, owed her life to the simple fact she had forgotten her glasses. She had been sleeping at her daughter's house in another part of the town and had gone back to her own home at 2 East Street, to see if there were any letters for her. She found a letter on the doormat from her son who was in the Merchant Service. Because she had forgotten her glasses she left the house. As she closed the front door she heard the familiar sound of German aero-engines over the Channel. She hurried down the road and within two minutes her house received a direct hit and was demolished. She said later: "If I had had my glasses with me I should have stopped there to read my son's letter and would probably have sat down to write an answer."

In the adjoining house, 1 East Street, Mrs H. Harris and her five children, aged from seventeen years to eighteen months, heard the raiders' engines and just managed to reach the coal cellar under the stairs when the house next door was hit. The upper part of her house was seriously damaged. Mrs Harris and her children were able to walk out of the wreckage unaided.

Another bomb fell outside in the road close to St Peter's Church and School, where a gas-main was fractured. The church lost its stained-glass windows and most of its roof, as did the school.

Wednesday 9th April. *0325 hrs — HEs — District affected — Alder Road. 3 houses demolished, 2 houses partially demolished, 8 houses seriously damaged, 32 houses slightly damaged. Casualties 1 male injured.*

A swift "Tip-and-run" attack was made in an area where Salter's Laundry had been wrecked last August. This time bombs fell on 25 Alder Road, where Mr and Mrs H.J. Hoile were living, although at the time of the raid they were staying in another part of the town. One bomb fell in the front garden of 41 Alder Road where the occupants, Mr and Mrs Taylor and a Miss Franklin, were fortunately in the back of the house.

A large number of motorists from outside Folkestone were being summoned for entering the town without displaying a yellow "Civil Defence" permit on their vehicle. When Captain Henderson was stopped by a constable in Sandgate Road he was not amused. He told the constable: "I'm an officer — I thought I was all right."

Charles Taylor, a 68-year-old fisherman, was machine-gunned for the third time. A Spitfire intervened but was shot down just outside the harbour. The pilot swam ashore and was met by soldiers.

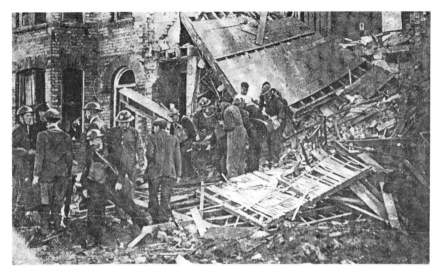

A dairy and butchers shop were wrecked in Guildhall Street during a "Tip-and-run" raid on 15th August 1942.

Saturday 26th April. *1315 hrs — HEs — District affected — Geraldine Road — St Hilda Road — Shorncliffe Crescent — field near water pumping station, Cherry Garden Lane. Casualties 4 female injured, 3 children injured.*

An Observer Corps post alerted the ack-ack who managed to put up a barrage of shells in front of seven Messerschmitts who were approaching Sandgate at sea level. Three of them veered off to release their bombs into the sea, while the other four reached Cheriton where they released their bombs simultaneously. These mid-day raids were becoming a feature of Luftwaffe policy and were usually intended for RAF Hawkinge. The Messerschmitt fighter-bomber became slow and vulnerable in that particular mode and pilots jettisoned their bombs at the slightest threat to their own safety.

Sunday 11th May. *0300 hrs — IBs — District affected — Varne Road — Hasborough Road — Wear Bay Crescent. 2 houses seriously damaged by fire, 2 houses slightly damaged by fire. Casualties nil.*

Incendiaries were dropped in the East Cliff area by a returning bomber. A RED Alert was in progress and all the missiles fell on military occupied houses — 10 Wear Bay Crescent, 20 Hasborough Road, 6 and 7 Varne Road. The civilians had been moved out. AFS teams arrived from Gladstone Road and the East Cliff Incinerator site.

Maltby's showrooms in Sandgate Road was displaying a yellow-nosed Messerschmitt Bf109 fighter, part of an exhibition.

90

Friday 16th May. *1915 hrs — Machine-gunning — District affected — Odeon Cinema, Sandgate Road. Casualties 1 male injured.*

People queuing outside the cinema to see Victor McLaglen in "Diamond Frontier" dived for cover when bullets and cannon shells spluttered along the road. They missed death by inches.

Thursday 29th May. *0210 hrs — Parachute mines — District affected — Morehall Avenue — Cherry Garden Avenue. 26 houses demolished or partly demolished, 40 houses seriously damaged, 560 houses slightly damaged. Casualties 5 male killed, 7 female killed, 1 child killed, 16 male injured, 23 female injured, 4 children injured.*

The German bomber crews' target was Folkestone West Railway Station which they missed by about 1,000 yards. The net result of their special skills was one of carnage when sleeping civilians took the brunt of the attack.

The bomb-doors of the Heinkel 111 opened as the familiar outline of the town was just a smudge on the edge of a glistening English Channel. The bomb-aimer in the nose of the aircraft watched the dark smudge creep towards the centre of the bomb-sight lens, around which were thin black lines marked in degrees. Behind him hung two black, sinister Luftmines carrying 500 kilo of explosive each. A parachute was attached to each mine to slow its rate of descent which minimised the accuracy of the missile. In the magnetic mode and dropped in coastal waters, for which it was originally designed, there was no need for such accuracy. Height was the important factor to make an accurate strike on a particular target. The bomber carrying the device needed to be under 1,000 feet, for when the parachute activated, the land-mine had already covered half the distance to the target.

The Mayor and Mayoress of Folkestone, George A. Gurr, JP and Kate M.J. Gurr, were among those killed when the first land-mine drifted onto houses in Morehall Avenue. They were killed instantly. Their bodies were not recovered from the mass of rubble, of what remained of their home at No.30, until several hours later.

Among the dead was an eighteen-month-old baby boy and his mother,. 24-year-old Betsy May Knott, who were living at No.28 with Daisy Crump, who also died.

There was extensive damage over a wide area to private houses and shops. Many people were rendered homeless through the terrible blast effect of the explosion. While rescue parties worked stealthily, searching among the splintered rafters and blocks of masonry for persons believed to be trapped, some householders in their night-clothes searched for missing pets.

The searching teams were further hampered by the extreme darkness. Enemy aircraft could still be heard overhead and auxiliary lights of any description could not be used. Also overhead was a young woman and her baby, marooned at the top of one house. She was standing on the smallest of ledges which spanned a chasm, once the front of the building. Her terrified cries for help sent

Shop fronts were wrecked when a bomb exploded in Cheriton Road on 18th August 1942, narrowly missing the Central Station just one hundred yards away.

shivers down the spines of rescuers below. They laboured to make way for the 50-feet wooden escape ladder which had arrived from the Dover Road Fire Station. Mother and baby were brought down to safety but recovering those people buried was a slow process. An elderly lady, a cripple, was heard calling from the back of her house. She was evidently trapped beneath tons of rubble when the sides of her house collapsed upon her.

Police Constable Spain, already decorated for bravery in an earlier incident, went to her assistance without a second's thought to his own safety. With extreme and meticulous dexterity, he dragged the woman out while others were supporting a makeshift tunnel.

PC Spain was recovering his breath, leaning against the wheel of the escape ladder, when a warden told him they had seen a body lying on a strip of flooring. It was Police Sergeant E. Swann, who had been sleeping in the same house as the Mayor and his wife. Except for just part of one wall nothing else remained standing and the Mayor's son-in-law was lying on a piece of flooring which hung at a ridiculous angle. When PC Spain reached the body he did not recognise the sergeant at first, but happened to notice the police armband, covered with plaster and dust and hanging on the corner of a fireplace.

Sergeant Swann had not regained consciousness when he was taken to hospital. Other fatal casualties included a well-known hotel porter and his wife, Herbert and Edith Archard, found at No.22; Mrs Pitcher had been killed outright when most of No.25 collapsed into the street. Her husband Harry, a woodwork instructor at a technical school, was seriously injured and later died in hospital.

Along with dozens of others Tom Turner, a member of the Cheriton ARP team, was blown out of his bed by the explosion. Although only partly dressed he clambered out of his wrecked home and joined the rescue teams in Morehall Avenue.

At first light the full extent of the damage was revealed. Everywhere lay hose-pipes dribbling water, fractured gas mains were being attended to and a river of water ran down the street to find its own level.

Covered from head to feet in a fine dust the rescue teams sat on piles of rubble sipping hot tea from enamel mugs. Just a few feet from them were the bodies of Special Constable Charles Jones, 25-year-old Florance Marsh and James and Winifred Sinstadt, all covered with official-looking grey blankets. The rescuers sat in silence, each wrapped up in their own thoughts. The word "incident", later to appear in the ARP record book, seemed dry, remote and colourless. Ernie Wakefield remembered the statement made by the Mayor last October, during a debate on whether to supply beds for people using air raid shelters. Ernie looked at the lifeless grey blanket and recalled: "Personally," George Gurr had said, ". . . I think it best to stay home in bed." The death of the town's Chief Magistrate and his wife shocked the townspeople deeply.

Saturday 31st May. *0135 hrs — Convoy attacked off Folkestone.*

Two German bombers were shot down during an attack on a convoy which ran the gauntlet of bombs and shells without loss whilst passing through the Straits of Dover in the early part of the morning. It was a brilliant moonlight setting and the dark outlines of the vessels could be clearly seen from the shore. People in the town were awakened by bursting shells, the rattle of machine-guns and the dull thud of bombs exploding. One German bomber came so close to the town that sentries and fire-watchers plainly saw the black crosses on the underside of the wings. The whole episode was illuminated by dozens of searchlights.

Saturday 7th June. *0038 hrs — HEs — District affected — East Cliff. Damage nil. Casualties nil.*

Thought to have been released by a German bomber returning to France, the single high explosive bomb made a deep crater near the Sanatorium.

Monday 9th June. *Fighter attacks.*

Several formations of Messerschmitt fighters were active over the coastal areas. The few AA defences were on Alert throughout the day although they were unable to pin-point any particular target. They engaged the fighter formations when they approached the town, some of which were only four in strength and flew from about sea-level to above 12,000 feet. Fortunately the only casualties seemed to be roofs and windows when bullets and cartridge cases fell over a wide area.

In peace-time Folkestone beaches would have been thronged with holiday-makers, the bathers would have been enjoying the cool sea in their hundreds and the Leas would have been crowded with people in summer attire. But the contrast in 1941 — the beaches are deserted, there are no bathers and the Leas, for all its smooth lawns, the beauty of its flower beds and the glorious sea views, even though seen through barbed-wire entanglements, was empty. At week-ends only the townspeople paraded along the Leas, the fewness of numbers somehow accentuated the sense of austerity and acute loneliness.

The German Air Force had suffered heavy losses over England since their offensive began in 1940 and their production lines failed to make up the losses. By June 1941 the enemy were concentrating on night intruder operations over England, to harass Bomber Command's operations when either taking off or returning to their airfields. German commanders had divided up British bases into three zones; East Anglia, Lincolnshire and Yorkshire.

As far as Folkestone was concerned in the strategic planning of such operations, all eyes were turned to the heavens in anticipation. During the daylight hours they watched our fighter formations hurtle over the Channel to attack targets in the Pas de Calais. At night, they heard our bombers heading for Germany. Searchlights probed the night sky, but our AA guns held their fire for fear of hitting our own aircraft.

Sirens continued to wail in Folkestone although there was a lull in enemy activity specifically aimed at the town. It clearly gave a well-earned respite to those who had experienced the precise damaged caused by high explosive bombs. Nothing can replace a shattered home, but much could be done to alleviate the hardship of those who found themselves suddenly homeless. As one report stated: "The discipline was impressive".

Wednesday 17th September. *2020 hrs — HEs — District affected — Subway adjoining Shorncliffe Road — Cheriton Road. Crater on footway, railway slightly damaged, 8 houses slightly damaged. Casualties 2 children injured.*

After the lull of three months this particular incident was the first since June and the last for 1941. It was just after 8 pm when a bomber followed the railway lines through the town. Estimated to be 250 kilos the bombs fell in a field behind the vacated Grange School where three calves were killed and another had to be destroyed later. One bomb fell on the footway, about sixty feet from the south side of the subway, where two young boys were sheltering. Albert Thompson of Wood Avenue, was taken to hospital suffering from a shrapnel wound, while his companion, Horace Long of Ivy Way, was treated for shock. Other bombs fell near Park Farm but little damage occurred.

1942

Friday 13th March. *2130 hrs — HEs — District affected — Ross Barracks — Chichester Road — Military Road. 1 barrack block seriously damaged, 1 garage, 1 tank hangar seriously damaged, 2 houses seriously damaged, 10 houses slightly damaged, 1 engine house demolished. Casualties 1 male injured.*

A single raider dropped a stick of bombs across Shorncliffe Camp. It was the first raid of 1942. A disused engine shed just disappeared when it received a direct hit. Another bomb exploded behind 31 Chichester Road, Sandgate, and brought the back of the house down, and nearby 29 and 33 were extensively damaged but there were no casualties there, although they were occupied at the time.

Thursday 2nd April. *2227 hrs — HEs — District affected — Wear Bay Road. Damage to windows of houses only. Casualties nil.*

All indications pointed towards a German bomber returning from an abortive mission and releasing its bomb load before crossing the English Channel. Some documents state there were two high explosive bombs dropped while others record three. In any event one of them cratered ground close to the railway tunnel just east of the Junction Station, and another exploded in the market garden complex of Messrs Pilcher and Chittenden, adjoining Wear Bay Road. The third allegedly detonated on the railway embankment.

Friday 24th April. *0836 hrs — HEs — District affected — Ship Street — Bradstone Avenue. No.4 Gasholder damaged, blast damage to houses. Casualties 1 male killed, 10 male injured, 16 female injured, 3 children injured.*

The Luftwaffe began their lightning "Tip-and-run" raids again. The Messerschmitts made their breakfast-time attack with speed and accuracy and had flown over the Channel at near nought feet. They were over the town before anyone knew what was happening. The gas company's holder at the rear of Bradstone Avenue was set on fire when a bomb exploded less than fifty feet away. It held about 700,000 cubic feet of gas, and when punctured by flying shrapnel, the gas ignited, sending flames licking up the sides of the holder.

Sid Lester recalled: ". . . our 10-year-old son Maurice had just left for school in Dover Road. My wife looked up from her dusting in the front room and saw a plane coming in low over the houses. She ran into the workshops where I worked and told me the gasholder, where Maurice had passed on his way to school, was in flames. 'The firemen won't let me through,' she said. I got on my bike and went to Dover Road School, hoping he would be there. Thank GOD! — he was, he had just reached St John's Street, when the bomb exploded. 'I saw it Dad! — I saw it!' he said, jumping up and down with excitement."

This 'News Chronicle' photograph of Ship Street was taken a couple of weeks after Messerschmitt fighter-bombers attacked the gasworks, on Friday 24th April 1942. Policemen were always on duty when furniture and household items were being recovered from bomb damaged dwellings. 99 Squadron ATC moved to this site in 1946, and remain there to this day.

Firemen tackled the flames which were finally stemmed at 10.30 am. But because of the high ground thousands of gallons of stagnant water cascaded down to Bradstone Avenue, where carpets and other household items rushed into the road.

Edith Winton, serving behind the counter at the corner shop in Boscombe Road, almost opposite the gasworks entrance, ducked behind the counter when a gas employee was blown through the glass door.

"More than sixty panes of glass were shattered," recalled Edith: "Pieces of shrapnel were embedded in the counters and staircase and tins of fruit, peas and beans were split open, their jagged edges looking like sharks' teeth. Mineral water was gushing onto the floor and broken jam jars were slowly sliding off a shelf. Sweet jars had smashed together but four dozen eggs under the counter had survived."

The bomb exploding outside 31 and 33 Ship Street caused extensive damage which spread into nearby Palmerston Street. The point of impact had fractured the gas main feeding the western district of the town and also broke a high pressure main to Hythe.

Despite the widespread damage affecting over 600 houses, only one fatal casualty occurred, and that was sheer bad luck. 52-year-old John Boss, a clerk at the employment exchange, had stopped to light his pipe outside the gasworks main gate. But then fate moves in mysterious ways. If he had waited until reaching Bournemouth Road before lighting his pipe he would most probably not have been killed.

Tuesday 5th May. *1820 hrs — HEs — District affected — Hook Close — Shorncliffe Road — St Hilda Road — Cavalry Lines. Extensive damage in all areas. Casualties 1 female killed, 10 male injured, 7 female injured, 5 children injured.*

The sea was as calm as the proverbial mill-pond with just a hint of mist hugging the contours of the beach. It was a natural phenomenon and as picturesque as the rising sun on a clear, calm morning. But this serenity was soon shattered when four yellow-nosed Messerschmitt fighter-bombers, in line abreast, made their entrance at Seabrook and shot over the roof-tops and up and over Hospital Hill before any gun crew had an inkling of their presence.

The intruders were no more than two hundred feet above ground when their cannon fire raked a London-bound train just leaving Shorncliffe Halt. The rear coach took most of the damage and half a dozen Royal Marines were injured. High explosive bombs were dropped almost simultaneously. 37-year-old Margaret Laker was killed when one 250-kilo bomb bounced through the walls of 158 Shorncliffe Road and exploded about four feet in front of No.1 Hook Close. Mrs Laker's husband and their 6-year-old son were in the rear of the house and sustained serious injuries.

Not far away another bomb went through the roof of No.1 Carter Road, then careered through the walls of Nos 2 and 3 before detonating on open ground near the railway track. Another exploded in the road outside Nos 3 and 4 St Hilda Road, and although there were no casualties here, four houses were badly damaged.

Private Green, sitting in the Services club room at the Cheriton Baptist Church, was slightly injured by flying wreckage which crashed through the roof. In all about twenty people received first aid of one kind or another, and the Shorncliffe Crescent Electricity Sub-Station was closed down for repairs.

Like many other incidents there was pandemonium for a few minutes then a strange silence prevailed over the whole area.

Sunday 17th May. *1008 hrs — HEs — District affected — Christ Church, Sandgate Road — Metropole Road East, Godwyn Road, Bouverie Road West. Christ Church demolished, 1 house demolished, slight damage to other houses. Casualties 1 male killed, 2 female killed, 21 male injured, 2 female injured.*

Unlike the German Baedeker raids which began in April, as a series of sharp reprisal raids on towns and cities such as Exeter, Canterbury and York, the "Tip-and-run" menace, although they were reprisals aimed at coastal towns, were considered more of a nuisance. The fuel capacity of the aircraft was the main consideration when coastal towns were selected for attack and most fell within a

When Beryl Vant joined the NFS in 1942, she was put on the telephone switchboard at Sandgate HQ. Rudimentary instruction caused havoc when plugs and wires became entangled with each other. Divisional Officer A. Woods was furious when he was connected to Bobby's Restaurant instead of the Control Room during an air raid!

radius of the Luftwaffe bases in the Pas de Calais. The results, as we have already seen, were sharp, isolated incidents of a disastrous nature.

One such incident happened on this Sunday morning when townspeople were preparing for church. In those days troops were obliged to attend church parades. On the Leas, troops were forming up into three ranks ready to be marched to Christ Church, while further down Sandgate Road, a column of army personnel were already marching towards the church. Meanwhile, almost clipping the waves, four Focke-Wulf fighter-bombers, each carrying a single 500-kilo high explosive bomb, headed towards their target. The German pilots, one can imagine, had become automatons — insensitive to their task outlined in the briefing room. Underneath them and perilously close was the bomb which had a delayed action fuse fitted to safeguard the aircraft at low altitude.

Although there was a look-out post manned by the army perched on top of No.1 Martello Tower above the Warren, it was the Observer post at Abbott's Cliff who spotted the gaggle of fighter-bombers. But even as they wound the field telephone handle it was too late.

Sixty-six-year-old Miss May Thompson, hard of hearing, who always arrived at church early to take her seat in the front pew, had arrived this Sunday even earlier than she had anticipated. Forty-seven-year-old Mrs Vera Ansell was carrying out the duties of verger and was distributing hymn and prayer books with Mrs Louisa Pearn.

The sun was high in the sky and there was a watery looking haze which obscured the cliffs. From almost nought feet the German pilots pulled back on their sticks to rise above the East Cliff. Bomb release catches set to the ON position they could see clearly the houses and streets ahead of them. Too low for the ack-ack guns on the Downs to engage them even if they could have seen them through the haze. The raiders were over the town now and released their bombs.

Christ Church erupted as one bomb made a direct hit. Only the tower remained standing as stonework and tiles flew in every direction. Just thirty yards away stood the Majestic Hotel, a well-known convivial watering-hole for the commissioned ranks of all three Services. Was it just a coincidence? — or were the German pilots aware of its existence?

The Pleasure Garden Theatre lost most of its windows when one bomb flattened 57 Bouverie Road West. In Godwyn Road three houses collapsed when a bomb bounced over Balfour Court in Sandgate Road, struck the road surface before bouncing a second time over Plain Road. It then struck the road in Bouverie Road West before finally exploding in Godwyn Road. From the first impact the bomb had travelled over 100 yards before detonating.

The fourth bomb penetrated the roof of the Grand Hotel and fell through three floors before coming out through the side of the building where it exploded in the road between the Grand and the Hotel Metropole. Although the Grand was unoccupied the Metropole was being used as an emergency hospital by the Royal Army Medical Corps. The explosion fatally injured 63-year-old Rowland Watkin-Edwards. He died in Victoria Hospital the same day, as did Mrs Ansell, recovered from beneath the rubble at Christ Church. Miss Thompson was killed outright by the explosion.

Making good the damage after these sneak raids caused problems in manpower. That evening a convoy of seven fire teams from Shoreham, Fishergate, Portslade, Peacehaven, Seaford, Hove and Brighton were on their way. They reached Folkestone at midnight. Sandgate Road was still strewn with rubble. Members of the Home Guard were clearing the rubble into Manor Road. Shakespeare Terrace was already obstructed by debris from Martin Walter's showroom. Hymn and prayer book pages had fluttered across the town like confetti, some being found over two miles away.

Saturday 30th May. *0437 hrs — HEs — District affected — Warren Halt Station. 60 feet of railway track displaced. Casualties nil.*
Four high explosive bombs were dropped with considerable accuracy upon the railway track between Folkestone and Dover. Repair crews were repairing the damage before first light and by 2.30 pm the line was open for business.

★

Christ Church, Sandgate Road, was built in 1850 without a clock tower, but it is the tower which still stands today after the rest of the church was demolished in May 1942, by Focke-Wulf fighter-bombers. Grave stones and gargoyles can be found in private hands in the Alkham Valley.

There was a lull in enemy activity during June and July, during which, with half an ear cocked for the first sign of trouble, a frenzied clean-up operation was begun. Damaged roofs and windows were repaired and a constant stream of lorries was shifting tons of rubble. Manor Road and Shakespeare Terrace were the first to be cleared after the bombing of Christ Church.

A man who did much to boost the morale of war-torn Folkestone was Arthur Kingdom, acknowledged as a fine musician and worthy of far wider acclaim than he ever achieved. He was known to thousands of people, both civilian and service personnel, as the organist at the Leas Cliff Hall. His 'Trio' appeared night after night featuring a very popular vocalist under the stage name of "Sylvia". With his great love of music Arthur would often squeeze-in an extra appearance on Friday evenings where, seated at the Compton organ at the Odeon Cinema, he would accompany the performers taking part in an amateur "Talent Night".

★

Of all the anecdotes and tales that go to make up this present work, all have been actual experiences and none are imagined. In some cases, however, the teller may seem to be inaccurate or have his dates mixed up, but this particular story, recalled by Eric Hart, portrays an event that did happen to him and his contemporaries.

"We at Shorncliffe Garrison formed the RE Platoon, Home Guard, under the watchful guidance of former Garrison Sergeant Major Hedges, himself then a white-collar worker on the civilian staff. His forthright word of command was lost on his allocation of 'Dad's Army'.

"During a military exercise in the area with units of the Regular Army as our adversary, a few of us took up a concealed position in a Pillbox on Sandgate Esplanade, perched on the edge of the promenade. At daybreak it looked as though our long vigil undercover was to be rewarded with the 'killing' of some opposing forces, as they warily advanced from the direction of Seabrook. With an umpire in the vicinity to record our success we waited with bated breath, our index fingers poised to pull the triggers. But then, just at that crucial moment when success seemed inevitable, a kindly lady, clad only in her dressing gown and bedroom slippers, came across the deserted road towards our pillbox.

"Carrying a tray laden with tea-pot and biscuit barrel, her trill 'Coo-ee' alerted our adversaries. We became the casualties."

6th June. *'Folkestone Herald':*
"Charles Arthur Holman, a 35-year-old member of the local Home Guard, married with two children, and only recently enrolled in the unit, was shot through the head during an exercise when Regular Army troops were firing live ammunition. Three Bren-guns were used to fire on fixed positions, in front of and on either side of the Home Guard contingent who were standing in three ranks. The exercise was often used in training programmes to enable troops to experience 'being under fire'. At the inevitable inquest an army officer gave evidence that a ricochet bullet was the cause of death. A verdict of accidental death was recorded." Charles Holman is not, however, mentioned on the Roll of Honour.

"It was announced at a council meeting that two stretches of Folkestone's fore-shore are to be opened to the public. The Parks Committee reported that the Regional Commissioner, in pursuance of directions issued by him under the Defence (General) Regulations, had approved for use by the public the following stretches of beach at Folkestone:
1. The beach at Sea Point, Sandgate.
2. The old bathing ground, East Cliff Sands.

The steady return home of Folkestone school children from South Wales was

Soon after the London Blitz of 1941, where water supplies dwindled to a mere trickle, pre-fabricated static water tanks were introduced in towns and cities, and erected at strategic positions. Coastal towns enjoyed the advantage of the sea, and in Folkestone, a bore-hole pump was installed in the Victoria Pier Dance Hall, pumping sea water to the bathing pool, both outdoor and indoor establishments, and also through a large-bore pipe network up to the town via the Leas Lift. Above: the NFS are constructing a small rail link to carry the bore-hole pump to the Victoria Pier Dance Hall floor, through which the pump was installed. (Kent Fire Brigade)

referred to at a council meeting. Alderman R.G. Wood said: "We all know that children are coming back in large numbers, and we are also aware that many down in South Wales today will not go back for the winter term." He continued: ". . . we don't know what lies before us in the coming year. We should take all steps possible to keep the children away. Not to do so would be a dereliction of duty."

Saturday 11th July

It was just after midnight when two shadowy figures left a small restaurant in Tontine Street and crept towards the harbour. Twenty-year-old Lorenzo Ogni and 18-year-old Nicodemo Vanucci, both British subjects of Italian parents, stopped beneath the railway arch leading to the fish market.

Fishing boats swayed at their moorings as the tide slowly lifted their bottoms from the mud. Ogni and Vanucci met no one, and saw no one, as they crept along the full length of the Stade. They knew where the sentries were. But had they been told that two boats would be moored on the outside of the East Pier, next to the East Cliff Sands?

They selected a boat called *Argonaut*, a small fifteen footer, complete with sail and a pair of oars. Under the very noses of sentries, policemen and fishermen, they cast off and quietly rowed over the minefield and out into the English Channel.

In the early house of 12th July, a signal was sent to the Admiralty from a Royal Naval destroyer at the head of a convoy going through the Dover Straits. By late afternoon, Ogni and Vanucci were being questioned by a security officer at Portsmouth. Ogni and Vanucci told him they hoped to reach France, make contact with the first German they saw and be repatriated to Italy to rejoin their families. Both agreed they had joined the Fascist Party in 1938, during a visit to Italy with their parents.

Charged with stealing a boat and unlawfully proceeding from the United Kingdom to a destination outside without leave of an Immigration Officer, contrary to the Defence Regulations, and further charged with unlawfully attempting voluntarily to enter enemy territory, they were brought back to Folkestone and appeared at the magistrates court.

Mr Robey, for the prosecution, asked the defendants: "Were you going to ask the Germans if they would be kind enough to return the boat? . . . Do you think they would bother themselves with a 15-feet punt belonging to a Folkestone fisherman?" Ogni answered impudently: "You never know."

The seriousness of their little folly lay in the comparative ease in which they left the country undetected. Had they not been spotted by one of our ships the implications loom into enormous speculation.

Ogni and Vanucci both received three months imprisonment.

Saturday 15th August. *1540 hrs — HEs — District affected — Guildhall Street — Church Street — Wellington Gardens — Manor House. 2 houses demolished, Borough Treasurer's Office demolished. Casualties 1 male killed, 1 male injured, 4 female injured.*

This was the first of the August 1942 air raids, when 500-kilo bombs were dropped by a small formation of FW190 fighter-bombers.

The most serious incident was in Guildhall Street where a bomb exploded in front of two shops — Nos 67 and 69. It was at No.67 where Mr John Fisher, a dairyman, was buried under the wreckage of his premises. He was dead when found. His wife Evelyn escaped with severe shock while other people in the shop were not seriously injured at all. The butcher's shop next door was unoccupied when the front of the building fell into the street.

Another bomb fell at the rear of Church Street, hitting a small building used by the staff of the Borough Treasurer's Office. It was completely destroyed and an underground air raid shelter also collapsed — although no one was inside! The main Corporation Offices close by suffered enormous damage as did the Central Cinema, where Virginia Bruce and Broderick Crawford in "Butch Minds The Baby" were being shown. The projector stopped and patrons filed out calmly into daylight to hear the siren wailing the "Alert".

Another bomb exploded at the rear of 15 Bouverie Road West, where Mrs Emma Ashdown was treated for severe shock. The fourth bomb fell on open ground at the back of the Manor Offices, Castle Hill Avenue, without causing any serious damage.

Being a Saturday a cricket match was in progress on the Cheriton Road Sports Ground, between a Police XI and the Royal Navy. Everyone threw themselves to the ground and spectators sought what little shelter they could find beside the

During the shell bombardment of Folkestone an area estimated at over 300 yards wide, starting at the harbour and reaching the Golf Links, was generally considered the most dangerous vicinity and became known as "Shell Alley". Above: shell blast damage was devastating at Clarence Street on 9th November 1942, where ten houses and two shops were demolished.

boundary wall. Thirty-six members of the regular police force left the sports ground on bicycles and motor-bikes to report for duty. When they failed to return the game was decided in favour of the Royal Navy!

Tuesday 18th August. *1651 hrs — HEs — District affected — Earls Avenue — Cheriton Road. 1 house demolished, 2 houses partly demolished, 39 houses seriously damaged, 9 slightly damaged. Casualties 3 male injured, 3 female injured, 1 child injured.*

It was a beautiful summer's evening when suddenly bombs were dropping everywhere. The aircraft were not identified and seemed to be flying very high. Fortunately there were no fatal injuries but there was a great deal of blast damage. A direct hit demolished 46 Earls Avenue, where Mr Wragg the gardener was seriously injured.

Another bomb, believed to have been of the anti-personnel type, exploded in mid-air in the vicinity of Sandgate and Shorncliffe. Little material damage was caused because the bomb had exploded about 4,000 feet above ground.

The biggest calamity was the result of a bomb exploding in the centre of Cheriton Road, about one hundred yards from the Central Railway Station, and near to the Brockman Road junction. Here a large crater broke all the main services including the sewer, which caused a complete stoppage of traffic in either direction. The fronts of a row of shops were completely wrecked.

In Howard's Store, business was proceeding as usual, customers were being served and assistants were busy when the bomb fell outside in the road.

Mrs Annie Woolcock, the assistant postmistress, was seriously injured when she was trapped by the feet when part of the floor collapsed. A girl assistant was treated for shock, but Mrs Hughes, who was in the small cashier's cubicle, was unhurt. Fortunately for Mrs Hughes the glass screens round the cubicle did not shatter. Alderman H. Hughes, the proprietor, was not more than 100 yards away when the bomb fell and escaped injury.

In the Central Tobacco Company's shop next door, Mr Fred Botsford was blown into the back of his premises, while Mr Jones at the chemist shop stood watching bottles falling from shelves as if a playful poltergeist had pushed them. Regular police augmented by auxiliaries and over fifty personnel from No.6 Rescue Party were on duty until about 9 pm.

Thursday 27th August. *1820 hrs — District affected — Shorncliffe Road — Jointon Road — Cheriton Road — Grimston Avenue — County Cricket Ground. 1 house seriously damaged, 25 houses slightly damaged. Casualties 1 male killed, 9 male injured, 1 female injured.*

There had been a steady increase in the establishment of light anti-aircraft guns in the south east of Kent, largely because of the "Tip-and-run" activities and to defend also the concentration of guns, searchlights and radar units which were scattered along the coastal belt.

This particular evening raid was similar to that of the 15th. The enemy formation was very high and one estimate gave a height of between 15,000 and 20,000 feet. The FW190s flew in over the town from a westerly direction and it was thought the number was about a dozen. There was some uncertainty because people were rushing about to take cover, although cricketers taking part in a match on the county ground adjoining Cheriton Road continued their game.

Folkestone Police XI were playing a team from a Field Ambulance XI of the RAMC, until the Chief Constable, R.C.M. Jenkins shouted "take cover", as a 500-kilo bomb screamed towards the pitch. The local police were batting at the time. Lance Corporal H.J. Harris was fielding at square leg when the bomb exploded near the wicket. He was killed instantly. Private C.D. Sinnock was seriously injured. Watching the game from the boundary Police Sergeant Alfred Gray was hit by shrapnel and sustained serious facial and head wounds. The Chief Constable was trapped when part of the stands collapsed.

It was perhaps fortuitous that No.5 First Aid Post personnel were based at the cricket ground. Their prompt medical treatment to the injured was commendable but despite their professionalism Police Sergeant Alfred Gray lost an eye.

Official records state the fighter-bombers were probably aiming for the railway track. As this particular raid was made from a great height it can be assumed that accuracy required to hit such a narrow target was considerably reduced.

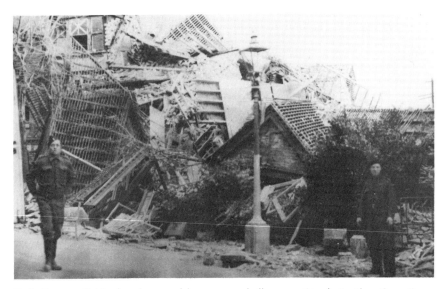

Both German fighter-bombers and long-range shells were aimed at either the railway viaduct or the gasworks. Although there was considerable disruption of gas services and rail time tables, neither were demolished. Above: these houses in Boscombe Road collapsed under a shell explosion aimed at either the viaduct or gasworks on 10th December 1942.

In hindsight it can also be assumed the pilots were aware of the heavy ack-ack guns recently installed at Capel, the battery firing for the first time (two rounds) three days before! German intelligence at least was accurate.

The 500-kilo bombs fell on either side of the railway by a considerable margin. One hit an ornamental pond in the garden of "Corner House" at the junction of Shorncliffe Road and Jointon Road. Another exploded on an allotment close to Grimston Avenue, and yet another fell at the rear of 71 and 72 Shorncliffe Road. There was extensive blast damage but no one was injured in these areas except for Colonel Ralph Mackie who received a slight cut to the head when a tile fell off his garage roof!

Wednesday 23rd September. *1440 hrs — Land-mine — District affected — Royal Pavilion Hotel. Casualties 3 male killed, 1 male seriously injured.*

Four workmen repairing war damage at the Royal Pavilion Hotel near the harbour just walked into a minefield in the gardens of the hotel. A mine exploded causing instantaneous death to 37-year-old Frederick Cooper, and seriously injuring 57-year-old Thomas Pepper and 40-year-old William George Warner, both of whom died of their injuries later at the Royal Victoria Hospital.

At the coroners inquest Henry Percy Morgan said he was in charge of men who were looking for a drain pipe in the hotel grounds. He insisted that no one informed him there were mines in the vicinity. When he heard the explosion he thought it was a gun.

One of the injured said they had just opened a sewer to find the main drain. Patrick Joseph Walsh went on: ". . . we could not locate it so we went outside to find it. We came to a window where there was a stone balustrade, Cooper was leading, Warner came next then Pepper and I came last. We decided to get down into a pit which was not closed by barbed wire. Warner was standing on some sandbags close to the window. I was about to follow him when there was an explosion."

The tragedy resulted in awards for bravery conferred upon two policemen and a civilian. The 'London Gazette' of Friday 18th December 1942, gives the official intimation of the awards and also contains an expression of commendation for brave conduct by War Reserve Constable William Charles Stockbridge of the Folkestone Borough Police Force.

The George Medal, the highest award for civilian bravery, was conferred upon Police Constable Cyril Ashley Williams, of the Folkestone force, and Mr George Fenton, a carpenter then living in Dolphins Road, Folkestone.

The citation reads: "Whilst on patrol duty Police Constable Williams heard an explosion and, on arriving at the scene, was called into a building and told that workmen had inadvertently gone into a part of the grounds that was mined. He saw an injured man lying on the ground some distance away. Williams, although aware of the great danger from other mines, immediately went to the casualty and carried him into the building. Fenton, who was also engaged upon work in the building, on hearing the explosion and seeing another man lying unconscious in the grounds, unhesitatingly climbed out of a basement window and traversed the mined area. He reached the victim and suceeded in carrying him to safety. Fenton and Williams showed great courage and complete disregard of their own personal safety."

Saturday 26th September. 2000 hrs — Combined Military/Civil Defence Casualties Services Exercise.

At 8 o'clock in the evening the whole of Folkestone came under an umbrella of intense activity when police, military, NFS, ARP and civilian volunteers took up their pre-selected positions in an exercise to test proficiency in locating and dealing with hundreds of pseudo-casualties.

The exercise was split into four separate attacks, totalling twenty-four incidents, each having a "real" potential where umpires closely watched the teams involved. They recorded from the outset the time it took for a particular service to attend the incident and how long before the casualties were found and dealt with.

Under the command of Colonel Gardner, the 192 Field Ambulance Unit, stationed at the Hotel Metropole, was heavily engaged in the operation and, although sixteen policemen were designated "casualties", the rest were soldiers in uniform. Many of them were "hidden" beneath cleverly erected debris in the

By the time the German long-range guns had been captured in September 1944, the cluster of small dwellings and tiny streets behind Tolputt's Timber Yard had been wrecked beyond recognition. Above: this picture covers only a small part of the shell damage to Saffron's Place, on 9th November 1942.

profusion of partly demolished dwellings in the town, while others were "planted" in some obscure positions.

Once the "casualties" had been satisfactorily dealt with they were required to dash to the next incident. And so by midnight fifty soldiers and sixteen policemen had each been in four separate incidents, ranging from Sandgate to the Junction Station; had been subjected to spurious forms of first aid; had been roped to stretchers and lowered out of windows; had been hauled up from basements and had been carried to nearly every Warden's Post in the borough. Half an hour after midnight the exercise drew to a close.

Exhaustion showed on the faces of many of the participants, but gallons of hot tea were dispensed by the mobile vans of the WVS, the NAAFI and the Salvation Army. As in every operation of this magnitude there are always one or two anecdotes which survive. One in particular has never been forgotten and concerns two soldiers who were "casualties".

The two soldiers in question had been "placed" in a derelict building to await their discovery in the first attack. When no one arrived to deal with them they pocketed their bandages and left for the nearest public house. Umpires comparing their notes afterwards discovered two casualties missing! A search was immediately implemented of all the known "casualty-sites" but to no avail. Then a message was received from the guardroom at Shorncliffe Barracks. It appeared that the two soldiers, extremely inebriated, having been thrown out of the hostelry at closing time, were making their way back to the "casualty-site" when they were picked up by the Military Police!

Monday 5th October. *2015 hrs — Shelling — District affected — Customs House — Southern Railway Pier — Bradstone Avenue. 7 properties seriously damaged, 243 properties slightly damaged. Casualties 2 male killed, 2 male injured.*

Shortly after the Dunkirk evacuation huge railway guns, running on existing French railway tracks, began operating in the Pas de Calais. At first these long-range guns were to provide the heavy bombardment necessary to dominate the Straits of Dover, but in 1941 and 1942 more permanent installations were being erected. Huge concrete casemates eventually held formidable artillery in various calibres.

Batterie Lindemann at Sandgatte for example, with its three 406-mm Krupp guns, was classed as the most intimidating of the twenty-four naval gun batteries installed between Calais and Boulogne. Grosser Kurfurst and Todt were other important installations but, during 1941 and 1942, our own artillery regiments had been confident that they could silence the German guns by their own bombardment. It was perhaps wishful thinking on their part for even as early as October 1940, the German guns accurately shelled British convoys more or less at will.

The German batteries enjoyed superiority both in equipment and in instant retaliatory capability, which was coupled with an uncanny accuracy.

Our own Siege Regiment long-range guns installed between Dover and St Margaret's were active in the counter-bombardment role but, while most of the British action concentrated upon enemy shipping, the Germans shelled our coastline indiscriminately, which condemned the civilian population to a new terror.

Three shells exploded on the town at about 8.15 pm and were the first since March 1941, when the Shorncliffe Garrison gymnasium had been hit. At the time a large formation of British bombers was heard flying out over the Channel towards France. A gun duel was also in progress between the German and our own Dover based artillery. A German shell struck close to the Customs House in the harbour with another exploding on the railway track on the Southern Railway Pier, about fifty yards from the lighthouse. The third shell fell in the rear garden at 42 Bradstone Avenue. All the casualties were military.

Saturday 31st October. *2020 hrs — HEs — Machine-gunning — District affected — Park Farm area. Blast damage to 150 houses, train blown up at Westenhanger. Casualties 2 male injured.*

In the afternoon a couple of Focke-Wulf 190s, probably encouraged by an overcast sky, flew in low over Cheriton and followed the railway track out towards the west. Just beyond Westenhanger they raked a train with their 20 mm cannon shells. The engine boiler blew up just as one of the fighters was overhead. The German fighter disintegrated into a thousand pieces. Fifty-five-year-old Walter Edwards, the engine driver from Ramsgate, was seriously

Although the charge required to send a heavy shell over the English Channel was very powerful the blast damage of the detonating shell depended largely on the type of building it had struck. Above: the Congregational Church Hall in Tontine Street was hit on 9th November 1942, and the roof was covered with corrugated iron sheets. The resulting blast was contained within the walls.

injured and taken to the Royal Victoria Hospital, where he died on 4th November.

Just after 8 pm the searchlight at Park Farm switched on as enemy bombers flew overhead. It became a target for three well-aimed bombs which caused considerable damage to houses in Walton Gardens, Downs Road, Dolphins Road and Mead Road. Two soldiers were taken to hospital at the Hotel Metropole suffering from shock.

Monday 9th November. 2022 hrs — Shelling — District affected — Dover Street — Clarence Street — Tontine Street — East Cliff South Quay. 10 houses demolished, 2 shops demolished, considerable blast damage. Casualties 2 male killed, 12 male injured, 6 female injured.

The Police Incident Report reads:

"
FOLKESTONE BOROUGH POLICE
Operational Report — Shelling Incident — 9th November 1942

Nature of incident

At 8.22 pm on Monday 9th November 1942, the first of seven shells fired at Folkestone from the French coast landed in Dover Street, and the shells arrived here at varying intervals until about 9.10 pm. Three of the shells landed in Dover Street, one in Clarence Street district, one in Tontine Street district, one at the bottom of the cliff near the East Cliff Sands and one near the South Quay, in the harbour.

Extent of damage

Heavy blast damage was occasioned and so far the extent is not definitely known, but it is believed that this is the greatest amount of blast damage so far suffered. Ten houses and two shops were demolished, whilst the roof and glass damage is very considerable. A small rowing boat was sunk in the harbour.

Casualties

Killed

William Baker	(17)	—	46 Clarence Street, Folkestone.
Robert Simpson	(60)	—	19 Clarence Street, Folkestone.

Seriously injured

Miss P. Brazier	(18)	—	52 Clarence Street, Folkestone.
Alfred Moull	(62)	—	48 Clarence Street, Folkestone.
Frederick Smith	(17)	—	50 Clarence Street, Folkestone.

Slightly injured

Henry Hobday	(63)	—	50 Clarence Street, Folkestone.
Samuel Williams	(59)	—	31 Tontine Street, Folkestone.
Herbert Rising	(28)	—	18 Tyson Road, Folkestone.
Sidney Baker	(14)	—	46 Clarence Street, Folkestone.
Ada C. Smith	(53)	—	44 Clarence Street, Folkestone.
Edmund Harris	(32)	—	104 Dallas Brett Crescent, Folkestone.
William Smith	(56)	—	44 Clarence Street, Folkestone.
Barbara Smith	(14)	—	44 Clarence Street, Folkestone.
Elizabeth Baker	(58)	—	96 Clarence Street, Folkestone.
Mrs Mabel List	(33)	—	40 Clarence Street, Folkestone.
Grace List	(12)	—	40 Clarence Street, Folkestone.
George Prescott	(45)	—	13a Hill Road, Folkestone.

Military casualties

Seriously injured

George List	(39)	—	40 Clarence Street, Folkestone.

Slightly injured

Samuel Battersby	(26)	—	St Andrew's Home, Folkestone.
Cecil Gosby	(28)	—	"La Maisonette", Eythorne.

Services engaged

Control Room

A depleted staff augmented by Regular Police was engaged from 8.25 pm until 11.30 pm.

Police

33 members of the Regular Force and Auxiliaries were engaged until 11 pm.

Casualty Services

First Aid Parties from Nos 2 & 5 Posts were engaged and the work performed at No.2 Post, where most of the casualties were treated, was most praiseworthy.

Rescue Party Personnel

In 1938 ARP training had become part of police qualifications and police instructors were engaged in examining civilians who were eventually to form the nucleus of the Civil Defence Force. Above: Police Constable Alfred Gray, who joined the Borough Force in 1929, became one of the first instructors. On 27th August 1942 he lost an eye whilst playing cricket at the Cheriton Road sports ground, during a "Tip-and-run" raid by Focke-Wulf 190s.

Folkestone "Clippies" employed by the East Kent Road Car Co. were a feature of the town's war years, not often remembered.

Parties from Nos 1 & 3 Depots were engaged and worked strenuously under difficult conditions to extricate persons trapped under damaged buildings, and clearing away debris.

Wardens

There was a full muster of wardens on the scene in very quick time and the assistance rendered by them in transmitting messages to the Control Room etc, was most valuable.

Incidents reported

(1) Bottom of Dover Street	—	By a warden	at 8.30 pm.
(2) Dover Street	—	By police	at 8.40 pm.
(3) Dover Street	—	By police	at 8.43 pm.
(4) East Cliff Sands	—	By special constable	at 8.58 pm.
(5) Clarence Street	—	By a warden	at 9.10 pm.
(6) Tontine Street	—	By police	at 9.30 pm.

Homeless persons

Twenty-eight persons were rendered homeless and were accommodated for the night in a rest centre (Baptist Chapel, Rendezvous Street), and all were found alternative accommodation by 2 pm 10th instant.

Shelters

Whilst the shelling was in progress considerable use was made by members of the public of all shelter accommodation.

Summary

The shells landed here whilst our heavy guns were firing at the French coast. No air activity was in evidence at the time and no warning in operation.

All CD Services worked smoothly with marked collaboration.

Confidential to: R.C.M. JENKINS,
The Chairman and Members   Chief Constable, and
of the Emergency (Civil   ARP Sub-Controller.
Defence) Committee."

Tuesday 10th November. 2259 hrs — Shelling — District affected — seawards of Folkestone Harbour — Harbour Arm. Casualties nil.

A number of shells aimed at Folkestone fell short of their target and landed in the sea.

Wednesday 11th November. 2235 hrs — Shelling — District affected — Folkestone Golf Links. Buildings occupied by military demolished. Casualties 4 soldiers killed, 3 soldiers seriously injured.

This was the third successive night shelling. The ranging shot exploded on the long arm of the harbour but the second shell unfortunately made a direct hit upon the sleeping quarters of the Searchlight Battery on the Golf Links, killing and maiming the crew.

Rescue teams from other towns were often sent for when a more serious incident had taken place. Above: a mixed bag of ARP and NFS members from Hythe were pictured here taking a well-earned break whilst clearing debris in the Sandgate area.

Thursday 12th November. *0045 hrs — Shelling — District affected — open ground beneath Sugar Loaf Hill. Casualties nil.*

The German bombardment of the coastal towns was increasing but, unlike an air raid, there was no apparent warning except to see the gun flashes on the French coast. Even then it was unpredictable. Gun flashes were often seen when Bomber Command were engaged on their night operations. Within the first week of the increased shelling, posters appeared pasted on telegraph poles and vacated shop windows. The 'Folkestone Herald' carried the following message:

SHELL WARNING INTRODUCED IN FOLKESTONE

Arrangements have been made for a shell warning to be introduced in Folkestone — if necessary. The shell warning will be the ordinary air raid sirens sounded twice, at an interval of one minute. On hearing the warning people are advised to go to shelters. The "Danger of Shelling Passed" signal will be the "All Clear" signal — one long note — sounded twice at an interval of one minute. For the present the shell warning will be sounded on three sirens only, those at the Grand Hotel, St Saviour's and the Electricity Works.

Sunday 15th November. *Church bells!*
On this Sunday church bells in Folkestone rang out for the first time since they were silenced in 1940 when invasion seemed imminent. Special permission had been granted for the church bells to be rung throughout the whole country in ". . . joyful acclaim of the success of the British Army in Egypt." Even the surviving bell hanging in Christ Church tower rang out with the rest in almost open defiance above the ruins, wrecked by a bomb seven months earlier.

Sunday 29th November. *1543 hrs — Machine-gunning — District affected — west end of town. Casualties nil.*
No further information available.

Thursday 10th December. *2127 hrs to 2328 hrs — Shelling — District affected — Inner harbour — Dover Road (Co-operative Stores) — Gas Works — Radnor Park Road — Boscombe Road — Spring Terrace — Royal Victoria Hospital. Widespread damage. Casualties 1 female killed, 4 male injured, 5 female injured, 1 child injured.*
It was just after 9.15 pm when the shelling began. The "range-finding" salvo went into the sea and the next fell into the inner harbour area. The salvo which followed put a shell behind the Ritz Dance Hall, Dover Road, and another blew out one end of Spring Terrace, which also shattered the Co-operative Stores almost opposite. Most of the people who had been in the Ritz had by then left, but the thrusting finger of fate pointed towards Mrs Gertrude Cohen and her pet dog "Paddy". Both were killed by flying masonry. Other shells fell near the gas works and demolished Nos 6 and 8 Boscombe Road, while another wrecked Nos 13 and 14 Radnor Park Road.

Friday 11th December. *0100 hrs to 1300 hrs — Shelling — District affected — The Bayle. Casualties nil.*
Although two high-calibre shells are listed as exploding on The Bayle, another document states South Street.

Tuesday 22nd December. *10.15 hrs — Machine-gunning — District affected — Town Centre. Casualties nil.*
No further details available.

Mrs Cohen and her little dog "Paddy" were both killed when a shell exploded in Dover Road, on 10th December 1942. Above: plate-glass windows are being replaced with plywood sheets at the Co-operative Stores which received extensive damage.

Just another thirty yards and this shell would have fallen on the Victoria Hospital. Instead, it demolished these two houses in Radnor Park Road, on 10th December 1942.

1943

Sunday 3rd January. *1452 hrs — HEs — District affected — Foreshore between Harbour Arm and Victoria Pier — Star & Garter grounds, Sandgate. 100 houses slightly damaged. Casualties 2 male injured, 4 female injured.*
The "Alert" sounded just before three o'clock in the afternoon. Radar installations spotted four "blips" on their screens at about 20,000 feet due east. Four FW190 fighter-bombers were coming in on a course almost parallel with the coastline. The ack-ack guns on the Downs overlooking the town opened fire. Shell bursts began to indicate the direction of attack and the smaller Bofors units recently installed also joined in, although the raiders were out of their range. As the aircraft altered course they then released their bombs, three of them falling harmlessly in the sea and one exploding in the grounds of the Star & Garter Home, Sandgate, now used by the NFS as their Headquarters. Falling just fifty yards behind Chichester Villas, it caused considerable damage to St Paul's Church and Sandgate School. Many people were rendered homeless by the blast effects and were soon accommodated at the homes of other residents in the area.

★

As 1,600 children had trickled back to the town it was debated at a council meeting whether further expenditure was necessary to up-date air raid shelters if it was decided to re-open schools such as Dover Road, Mundella, George Spurgeon, Morehall and Harcourt.

Sunday 17th January. *2020 hrs — HEs & IBs — District affected — Penfold Road — Warren Way — Radnor Bridge Road — Thanet Gardens — Lennard Road. 3 houses demolished, considerable damage. Casualties 3 male injured (including 2 war reserve constables), 1 female injured, 2 children injured.*
The "Alert" had sounded earlier in the evening when German bombers flew towards London. The ack-ack barrage was believed to be the most concentrated yet experienced in the area but even so, the bombers were flying into an even greater barrage on the outskirts of London. It is assumed that one raider turned back and released its bombs and incendiaries on Folkestone as it fled towards France.
Estimates reveal that ten high explosive bombs of the delayed-action type were dropped and several canisters of incendiaries. No.5 Radnor Bridge Road, then occupied by the Longhurst family, was soon alight when several incendiaries penetrated the roof. There were fierce fires started which

The German long-range artillery in the Pas de Calais enjoyed superiority in both equipment and instant retaliatory capability. Above: this picture shows the Customs House in the harbour, heavily damaged by shells on 5th October 1942.

eventually gutted the dwelling and the one next door. One report states that 50-kilo bombs, known as "Firepots", were an additional hazard when they fell in Rylands Place, Warren Road, Southbourne Road, Thanet Gardens and Dudley Road. Two of the delayed-action bombs fell in Lennard Road, one of which did not explode until 0045 hrs, while the other detonated at 0845 hrs on the following morning. This one blew Police War Reserve Constable Sacree off his bicycle. He, Mrs Greenstreet and Mr Rumsey were buried beneath the debris when Nos 1 and 2 Lennard Road just collapsed into the roadway. A number of local residents were moved to the Baptist Church, Rendezvous Street, where Lady Bomford and her helpers worked long hours to comfort the unfortunates.

Monday 18th January. *1945 hrs — HEs — District affected — Folkestone Harbour — the Bayle. 1 house demolished, Customs House demolished. Casualties nil.*
    A small formation of Junkers 88 bombers met a fierce ack-ack barrage when they approached the coast between Dover and Folkestone. They immediately split up and one turned towards the town. At no more than about 1,000 feet it was soon over the harbour with its bomb-doors open and its machine-guns firing. One bomb blew the Bondage Stores apart in a most spectacular fashion. Being empty at the time it just collapsed like a pack of cards. Another bomb demolished an unoccupied house called "Fairview" which had stood at the top of the Bayle steps. Altogether about 87 dwellings were heavily damaged by blast, including the offices of the 'Folkestone, Hythe & District Herald'.

★

On Wednesday 20th townspeople out shopping were quite deafened by the Capel 8-inch guns firing a salvo. After the first bang people stood to watch the huge sheets of flame leaping out of the barrels, followed by black smoke which almost obliterated the cliff-top from view. Seven shells were fired on this occasion but, within a week, just about everything closed down when the area saw the worst gales for ten years. There were tremendous seas running and on Saturday 30th there was a sharp electric storm. On the Sunday following there were torrential rain squalls and dozens of trees were uprooted in the town.

★

The gales and storms had subsided by the middle of February, but a number of people were startled to hear one evening the bell ringing in the tower of Christ Church. It was not long before a policeman investigated and found two small boys had found easy access to the belfry by an unlocked door in the tower!

★

Flowers on the Leas were a rare phenomenon now but the Parks Superintendent was growing leeks in the flower beds for the second year. He let them seed and during the winter months collected over eleven pounds of seed.

★

"DON'T TOUCH THESE BOMBS"
(BUTTERFLY BOMBS)

The public has already been warned in various ways of the danger of touching a small German bomb weighing about 4 lb. It is usually painted either greyish-green or a bright yellow. This bomb, known as the small anti-personnel bomb, may be found with the outer casing either open or shut. If shut, it looks like a large, round cigarette tin with a short, thick wire protruding from one side. If open, the outer casing expands into four hinged parts at the end of the wire. A number of these bombs have been dropped in the last few days and may be found scattered over a wide area. The public is warned on no account to approach or touch such a bomb but report it at once to the wardens or police. They are liable to explode at the slightest touch.

Tuesday 2nd March. *2101 hrs — Shelling — District affected — Harbour area — Harbour Hotel. Casualties 3 seriously injured, 2 slightly injured.*

One official document, the "Borough of Folkestone's Resumé of Enemy Action", confuses 2nd March with 12th March, and lists damaged buildings on 12th as having happened on 2nd. The "War Diary" however, states a salvo of three shells straddled the harbour railway station and the beach with one shell hitting the Harbour Hotel.

Many German long-range shells fell short of their target and were usually referred to as "ranging-shots". Each one was, nevertheless, recorded by the military observers who occupied strategic positions on the coast. With a height adjustment the next salvo of shells usually found its mark. Above: shells damaged the harbour and the Southern Railway Station until not one building was unscathed.

Friday 12th March. *0227 hrs — Shelling — District affected — High Street. Damage to World's Stores & Earl Grey public house — 'Folkestone Express' offices. Casualties 1 male injured.*

Only two shells fell on the town on this occasion. One detonated on the already demolished Bondage Stores in the harbour area while the other completely demolished the 'Express' newspaper offices in the High Street. Property on either side of the street was badly damaged with the blast taking out one complete side of the Earl Grey and also part of the World's Stores grocery shop.

Monday 5th April. *1035 hrs to 1625 hrs — Shelling — District affected — Mead Road — Harbour. 2 houses seriously damaged, 72 houses slightly damaged. Casualties 2 male killed, 2 male injured, 2 female injured.*

When a shell fell in the harbour vicinity the shell warning was operated at 0044 hrs. There were no reports of any damage but at 0227 hrs another shell exploded in the air above the harbour. As there was no further shell activity the "All Clear" sounded at 0319 hrs. But later the warning sounded again when the Dover guns began their reply.

Townspeople were undecided whether to vacate their shelters and climb back into their beds, or remain where they were when the "All Clear" sounded at

0428 hrs. By 0835 hrs Dover was receiving a pounding and most people lay in their shelters listening to the explosions. The final "All Clear" was given at 1017 hrs. Bleary-eyed and bad-tempered through lack of sleep, people turned up late for work. Then a shell exploded on the footpath between the rear of Nos 72 and 74 Mead Road and the allotments. Both houses were extensively damaged and a further 72 were shattered by blast.

Eighty-three-year-old Frederick Scott and 67-year-old Ernest Sayer had just reached their vegetable plots and both were killed instantly.

Friday 9th April. *1753 hrs — HEs — District affected — Dover Road — Archer Road — Ormonde Road — Wear Bay Road — Canterbury Road. 12 houses demolished, 24 houses seriously damaged, 250 houses slightly damaged. Casualties 2 male killed, 1 female killed, 8 male injured, 9 female injured, 3 children slightly injured.*

Bill Heaton of Dog 4 Post, Observer Corps, raised his binoculars when he thought he saw movement out over the Channel. Adjusting the focusing wheel he observed four FW190s close to the water and heading towards Lydden Spout. As the grey shapes altered course he shouted to his companion: "Four-One-Nineties approaching Folkestone!" As the message was transmitted to Control by field telephone there was a thirty second delay. In that thirty seconds the grey-camouflaged, red-nosed fighter-bombers were pulling up to clear the East Cliff. The four Jumo engines snarled in protest as each fighter-bomber, carrying a 500-kilo high explosive bomb, shot over the Junction Station. The 3.7-inch ack-ack guns at Crete Road East were unable to engage the raiders. They were flying too low. The recently installed 40-mm Bofors Light AA units, however, opened fire just as the siren sounded in the town. But they also were too late to be effective.

The German cannon shells struck houses and streets, then the bombs were released. Three people were killed: Mr and Mrs H.C. Hopper of 6 Archer Road, and Percy Willis, who was in Dover Road on his motorcycle. One cannon shell passed through his body killing him instantly. The bomb which destroyed the Hopper's home, first struck the roadway in Gladstone Road, scooping out some of the tarmac, then went through a wall before leaping up over the Co-operative Dairy to explode on Nos 6 and 8 Archer Road.

Mrs Skouse, daughter of the Hoppers, was fortunately out at the time of the raid, but that fact was unknown to the Rescue Unit. They eventually sent for a Casualty Detector Unit which arrived from Chatham.

St Saviour's Mission Hall was also damaged where a short time before a Brownie rally had been held. A Methodist Church, schoolroom and an ARP Wardens Post were also badly hit.

One of the bombs struck Nos 110 and 112 Dover Road, demolishing both and badly damaging 114. This was where Percy Willis, delivering produce from his Pay Street small-holding near Hawkinge, met his death. There were a number of trapped people including Mrs Florence Hall at 110 Dover Road. She was

Among the incendiaries dropped on 17th January 1943 were those known as "Fire-pots", containing a mixture of oil and flammable material which ignited on impact. Above: houses in Warren Road damaged by a "Fire-pot".

seriously injured and was one of the first to be rescued and taken to hospital. Four First Aid Units were engaged and one NFS pump was called from the Dover Road Depot to attend to a fire in one of the six shops damaged by blast.

In addition to the retail shops damaged the Martello Hotel, where the Local Authority Emergency Food Dump was stored, also received damage which buried the cache in rubble. The Martello had only recently been occupied by George Offen, who just a short while before had been shelled out of the Harbour Hotel in South Street.

Chief Inspector Holland, then in charge of the Folkestone Division of the Kent Constabulary, escaped injury by the skin of his teeth. He happened to be driving past the Ragland Hotel, Dover Road, when he glimpsed two of the raiders over the roof tops. He thought his car had been overturned when the blast of a bomb exploding sent his vehicle sideways, then he seemed to be enveloped in a dense fog. Further down the road he nearly knocked a woman down when she ran across the road in front of him.

Coming up the hill in the opposite direction was Eric Adams, a traveller for Messrs Olby's.

"Everything went dark for a few seconds and I was choked with dust and fumes" he said afterwards.

Another bomb exploded at the rear of 18 Wear Bay Road, the home of ex-councillor H. Franks. The fourth bomb burst at the junction of Ormonde Road and Tram Road, bringing down houses already previously damaged. Six rescue parties were deployed overall leaving just two in reserve. A reinforcement party arrived later from Bridge and was held in reserve at the Sidney Street Depot.

Saturday 1st May. *2247 hrs — Shelling — District affected — junction Brockman and Claremont Roads — West Cliff Gardens — Esplanade Hotel. Damage to surrounding property. Casualties nil.*

Shelling was usually confined to a narrow strip of no more than a quarter of a mile wide, starting seaward of the harbour and ending on the Golf Links. The early bombardments wrought serious havoc upon certain areas of the town which had widened towards the end of four years harassment.

The shell which fell in the roadway at the junction of Brockman and Claremont Roads dislodged the gas main and sent a huge spire of flame upwards to a height of forty feet. The Hotel Esplanade lost all its windows when the second shell exploded in the garden, leaving a crater large enough to swallow a double-decker bus. Had the shell reached another thirty yards and exploded in Sandgate Road it might have swallowed an East Kent bus at the terminus opposite Bobby's.

Tuesday 25th May. *2155 hrs — HEs — District affected — Foreshore and Marine Gardens. Minor damage. Casualties nil.*

This incident has been recorded as the last daylight "Tip-and-run" raid made on Folkestone by Focke-Wulf fighter-bombers. The CO of No.91 (Nigerian) Squadron, Squadron Leader Ray Harries, DFC, based at RAF Hawkinge, was about to land at the airfield with three other Spitfires when an order to "scramble" came over his radio. Fifteen "Bandits" had been monitored on local radar installations heading for Folkestone. The new Griffin engined Spitfires shot away from the airfield boundary like bats out of hell. They met the raiders about one mile from the harbour. The German pilots were taken by surprise and jettisoned their 500-kilo bombs hurriedly into the sea, although one of them fell onto Marine Gardens setting off a number of land-mines which damaged the Boating Pool.

The 20-mm cannons of the Free French pilot Maridor made short work of the leading FW190 which almost immediately spun into the sea with a terrific full-boosted dive sending great plumes of spray into the air. Harries, the CO, reached two fleeing fighter-bombers and shot both down while a new pilot to the squadron, Pilot Officer Round, raced after another raider and eventually caught it three miles from the French coast where it blew up.

Five enemy aircraft were credited to the squadron without loss to themselves. They became heroes that night. The Chief Constable telephoned the airfield thanking the squadron for saving Folkestone from what might have been a disastrous incident. Telegrams and letters followed and, on 3rd June, a reception in their honour was held at Bobby's restaurant. Later Nigeria bestowed twenty-four silver tankards on the unit in tribute to their gallant action.

A salvo of three shells almost demolished the Harbour Hotel and took out the back wall of the London and Paris Hotel at 8 o'clcok on the evening of 2nd March 1943. By the end of the war South Street, near the harbour, received damage that was unrepairable.

Tuesday 22nd June. *0236 hrs — HEs — District affected — Cheriton Road junction with Cornwallis Avenue — Golf Links — Alder Road — 200 yards NW of Valiant Sailor public house — south of Crete Road on open ground. 120 houses slightly damaged. Casualties 1 male injured, 1 female injured.*

High explosive bombs were dropped during a period of considerable air activity lasting from 2.30 am to about 4.00 am. Enemy aircraft were not flying in formation and appeared to make sporadic attacks upon areas from a great height. Searchlights were seen operating from Canterbury, Dover and on the Romney Marshes. When an enemy aircraft was coned with searchlights the guns opened fire.

The first bomb fell on the pavement outside 134 Cheriton Road, the second narrowly missed the big guns at Capel and blew out every pane of glass in the Valiant Sailor pub. The next exploded on the Golf Links next to Alder Road where a special constable and woman were slightly injured by flying debris. Both were treated at the Sports Ground First Aid Post.

Monday 29th June. *0001 hrs — Shelling — District affected — Boscombe Road — Royal Pavilion Hotel grounds. 2 houses demolished, 2 houses badly damaged, 153 houses slightly damaged. Casualties nil.*

Sentries at the East Cliff gun site observed the flashes as the German long-range artillery opened fire just after midnight. Field telephones began to ring in the Control Room just as the first shell exploded on unoccupied houses in Boscombe Road, narrowly missing the gas holders. Ten minutes later another shell fell in the grounds of the Royal Pavilion Hotel. It set off dozens of land-mines in repetitive detonations.

Monday 5th July. *0320 hrs — Shelling — District affected — Dover Street. 2 houses demolished, 2 houses badly damaged, 5 houses temporarily made uninhabit-able, 117 houses slightly damaged. Casualties 2 male injured, 3 female injured, 1 child injured.*

The shell warning had sounded at 0223 hrs when a message was received that Dover was being pounded. One hour later a shell struck Nos 97 and 99 Dover Street, demolishing both dwellings and extensively damaging Nos 101 and 103. A heavy pump was called from the NFS Depot at Dover Road because a gaslight standard caught fire. Sixteen people were rendered homeless and sent to the "Binerton" Rest Centre, from where they were re-billeted during the day.

Saturday 4th September. *0015 to 0030 hrs — Shelling — District affected — Foreshore. Damage nil. Casualties nil.*

Only two shells fired from the French coast, during a Dover bombardment, reached the Folkestone area.

Tuesday 7th September. *0250 hrs — HEs — District affected — West Terrace — Road of Remembrance — Marine Parade — Lower Sandgate Road. Damage was caused to buildings already partly demolished from earlier incidents. Casualties nil.*

A cone of searchlights illuminated a single German bomber which released its bomb load immediately to take evasive action. The bomber turned towards France when heavy AA fire opened up.

Saturday 25th September. *0450 hrs — Shelling — District affected — Folkestone Harbour — The Durlocks Estate. 4 houses demolished, 100 houses damaged by blast. Casualties 2 children killed, 2 male injured, 4 female injured.*

The shell warning was sounded at 4.25 am, immediately following a similar warning in the Dover area. The first shell to reach Folkestone almost struck the Southern Railway Pier at 4.38 am. The second arrived at 4.40 am and brought with it the finger of death. It exploded amongst the Sir Philip Sassoon Housing Estate on The Durlocks — Nos 3, 4, 5 and 6 were wrecked. Police Sergeant Dolbear was moved to tears when 10-year-old Jean Pegden and her 2-year-old brother Derek, their little bodies still warm, were brought out from beneath the rubble, lifeless and covered in a fine dust. Their mother was brought out soon afterwards in an unconscious state. Military personnel from the St Andrew's Home, site of the Folkestone West Coastal Battery, attended the incident and worked shoulder to shoulder with the three rescue parties, as did Mr Cecil Bricknell who lived at 10 The Durlocks. By 7 o'clock that morning the three ambulances, the rescue parties, the wardens, police and military personnel had moved away from the pile of debris that once had been home to three families. A rag doll wedged between broken floorboards became an emotive symbol.

Only two long-range shells were aimed at Folkestone on the night of 12th March 1943, but one of them demolished the 'Folkestone Express' newspaper offices in High Street. Claude C. Crowhurst, later Editor of the 'Folkestone & Hythe District Herald', from 1940 to 1945 and author of the booklet 'Frontline Folkestone', was a former Editor of the 'Folkestone Express'. Above: the Earl Grey public house, seen on the extreme right of the picture, still stands today.

Sunday 3rd October. *0020 hrs — Shelling — District affected — in sea near harbour — rear of Clarence Street — rear of Bradstone Avenue — Park Farm west of brickfields. Gas Holder No.2 damaged, 350 houses damaged. Casualties 1 child injured.*

The shelling warning was sounded at 10.08 pm when our own big guns at Dover opened fire across the Channel. Enemy guns replied almost at once and shells fell in Folkestone until 1.30 am. The "All Clear" was sounded at 2.28 am.

The first shell fell near the harbour but the second exploded in the already damaged Clarence Street where twenty-five people were rendered homeless. They were taken to the Rest Centre at Pelham Gardens initially, but by 10.00 am that morning had been found billets in the town. Four-months-old Betty Taylor, of 8 Peter Street, was taken to hospital with shock and abrasions when the house was almost demolished by blast.

No.2 Gas Holder within the Gas Company's boundary caught fire when the third shell exploded nearby. Also set alight was a rotary scrubber and a wooden cooling tower, adjoining Broadmead Road. In his report on the incident Mr E.F. Smallbone, then engineer and manager of Folkestone Gasworks, wrote: "Numerous employees turned out to assist, and everyone, including the NFS

126

and the Company's Home Guard, on Fire Watch Duty, gave of their best under rather trying conditions." He continued his report in picturesque style: "The works resembled nothing so much as a Brocks Benefit Night, with fantail sprays of foam from the washer, escaping steam and roasted particles of foam descending like snow as extras." Shell splinters damaged other gas holders and one of them, with a water tank capacity of 1,250,000 gallons, leaked like a sieve. The last shell exploded harmlessly on open ground at Park Farm, where the searchlight battery personnel were blasted out of their beds.

Monday 25th October. 2155 hrs — Shelling — District affected — Road of Remembrance — Golf Links. Window damage only. Casualties nil.
A shell landed halfway down the embankment adjacent to the Road of Remembrance and cut off an electricity supply cable which served the Royal Navy's secret bunker. The other two shells fell about 300 yards east of Cherry Garden Avenue without causing any damage or injury.

Wednesday 3rd November. 2240 hrs — Shelling — District affected — junction of Cherry Garden Avenue and Hill Road. Damage nil. Casualties nil.
Although damage reports stated nil, a few pieces of shrapnel flew into houses in the vicinity. Our own guns had been firing at the Germans across the Channel and the enemy had replied within about fifteen minutes.

Saturday 4th December. 0316 hrs — Shelling — District affected — in sea off Copt Point — Cherry Garden Avenue — Dover Street. 1 troop carrier burnt out, 1 troop carrier extensively damaged, 2 houses badly damaged, 50 houses slightly damaged, Gordon Boy's Club damaged. Casualties nil.
A sentry gave the alarm when he observed the gun flashes from the French coast, but by the time a shell had arrived he had dived headlong into a sand-bagged trench. It was all the more regrettable when he became scarred for life. His tin hat was dislodged and cut into his scalp.
Two shells of the first salvo reached the Golf Links and another straddled two bren-gun carriers parked in Cherry Garden Avenue. Another exploded in Dover Street and blew out a wall of the Gordon Boy's Club, then used by the Sea Cadets. Unoccupied dwellings, 86 and 88 Dover Street, were rendered uninhabitable.

Tuesday 23rd December. 1950 hrs to 2230 hrs — Shelling — District affected — junction of Wear Bay Road and East Cliff Gardens — Foord Road — Tram Road — Radnor Park near viaduct. 1 house destroyed, 1 house seriously damaged, 1 shop seriously damaged, 200 houses slightly damaged, extensive damage to Tolputt's Timber Yard. Casualties 2 male injured.
The shell warning sounded at 7.50 pm when the Dover guns began firing across the Channel. The German reply started at 8.45 pm with remarkable accuracy. The first shell exploded just on the perimeter of the East Cliff gun

Estimated at 1,000 kilo, the bomb which damaged "Fairview" at the top of the Boyle steps left a large crater. It had been released by a low-flying JU88. A house has since been built on the exact spot.

battery near St Andrew's. The second shell actually burst in the air over East Cliff Gardens just after 9 pm wounding two army personnel who were on sentry duty at the Radnor Bridge Road barricade. The tall chimney at Tolputt's Timber Yard in Tram Road received a direct hit by a shell which went right through the base of the brickwork. If there had been a prize for marksmanship then the German battery commander would have undoubtedly been pleased to accept his trophy. As other shells fell all over the town at ten minute intervals people were apprehensive in the extreme, especially those in a shelter near Radnor Park when one shell exploded just a short distance away from them. The viaduct spanning Foord Road, its massive columns towering above small dwellings in New Street and Darby Road, miraculously withstood the shattering explosion of a near miss. Because it fell in soft ground it was at first believed to be unexploded. This resulted in 70 people being moved from their homes in the Foord and Darby Road areas to Rest Centres.

A five mile per hour speed limit was imposed upon trains using the viaduct until the Bomb Disposal Unit gave the all clear after digging down to 20 feet where they discovered evidence that the shell had exploded. People at Rye's Stores in New Street could have told them it had exploded. The shop practically collapsed under the effects of blast. A further five shells fell in the sea before the "All Clear" sounded.

1944

Thursday 20th January. *0447 hrs — Shelling — District affected — Bradley Road — Isolation Hospital — sea off Copt Point — Grange Road — St Winifred's Road — Danton Pinch. 1 house demolished, 14 houses seriously damaged, 200 houses slightly damaged. Casualties 1 male injured, 2 female injured.*

The Dover guns opened up a barrage of lethal missiles at the Germans which brought the shell warning into operation almost immediately. As was expected the German reply spread shells along the Kent coast from Deal to Folkestone. The first came into the town at 5.28 am and blew a hole in Bradley Road, the sound of the explosion reverberated around the houses before the whooshing sound of its arrival was heard. That phenomenon was a frightening peculiarity of shelling, anyone near an explosion would automatically bend double. No one had the slightest idea where the next would fall.

The second blew a twenty feet crater in the grounds at the Isolation Hospital near Creteway Down, then two plopped into the sea. The next salvo travelled further and reached Cheriton. Although a store and stables were extensively damaged in Bradley Road, the most serious damage occurred in St Winifred's Road, Cheriton, where Frank and Doris Bills at No.17 were buried beneath tons of rubble. It was here the Rescue Services concentrated when half of the dwellings received considerable blast damage, rendering many people homeless within seconds. The Rest Centre at Pelham Gardens was opened and a mobile canteen van, run by the Dover Salvation Army, produced gallons of hot tea to the police, ambulancemen, a gas repair party and rescue parties. Another rescue party attended Grange Road, Cheriton, where a shell demolished a house, fortunately unoccupied. The "All Clear" sounded at 0845 hrs.

Friday 11th February. *1950 hrs — HEs — District affected — Shorncliffe Crescent. 2 houses seriously damaged. Casualties nil.*

The drone of enemy aircraft engines was heard above the town. It was an overcast, still evening. Sentries and fire-watchers scanned the leaden sky for the first signs of activity. The projectors in local cinemas ground to a stop and there appeared on the screens a familiar message — "An Air Raid Warning Has Been Sounded". Few people left their seats. The evening's programme restarted.

Ernie Wakefield was driving his Austin three tonner along the Shorncliffe Road when above the engine noise he heard a bomb screaming. The Austin was approaching Shorncliffe Crescent when the bomb exploded. Ernie stopped the lorry and dived out of the cab into a nearby hedge. Slates and tiles ripped into the hedge around him but he was unscathed. He stood up and listened. There was an uncanny silence. It was as if he was the only person on the face of the

Folkestone fishermen, despite the many regulations imposed upon their businesses, not to mention the forced curfew when they were required to be back in the harbour before dusk, continued to fish between the mine fields throughout the war years. Like the barrage balloons over Dover, they became "fair-game" for German fighter pilots and were shot at on numerous occasions. Above: Folkestone fishermen Ginger Hogben and Frank Saunders are donating part of their catch to 91 Squadron pilots at Hawkinge, who routed Focke-Wulf fighter-bombers approaching the town on 25th May 1943.

('Kent Messenger')

earth. Cupping a lighted match with his hands he puffed on a battered cigarette, before driving on towards where the bomb had wrecked a couple of houses. He joined the rescue party and clambered over brick rubble searching for the occupants. It had become second nature to him — no one questioned him, it was as if he was part of their unit. They listened for the tell-tale signs of life — a call for help — a whimpering child. As the minutes passed they crawled under rafters and sloping floors to reach that one area of comparative safety — the staircase. Then a warden was heard to shout: "Stop Searching — House not occupied!"

Men from the Gasworks sealed off a fractured pipe but water ran down the road to find its own level.

Thursday 20th April. *2255 hrs — Shelling — District affected — junction of Joyes Road and Sidney Street. 200 houses slightly damaged. Casualties nil.*

Our own long-range guns had opened fire upon the German positions in the Pas de Calais and by 11.00 pm the shell warning was given. Only one shell fell on

the town and that penetrated eighteen feet below ground just behind 46 Joyes Road, and very close to an air raid shelter in which the occupier and his family were taking shelter. Because of the depth before detonating an unusually large amount of clay soil was displaced and scattered over a very wide area. The family said afterwards that they: "hardly noticed anything had happened."

Wednesday 24th May. *0132 hrs — Shelling — District affected — Alexander Street. 2 houses demolished, 2 houses badly damaged, 200 houses slightly damaged. Casualties 1 male killed, 1 female killed, 2 male injured, 4 female injured.*

The official Operational Report for this incident coldly states: "The shelling warning was sounded at 00.46 am, and the 'All Clear' at 2.58 am (0046 hrs to 0258 hrs!). British guns commenced firing and enemy guns replied soon afterwards.

"Rest Centre at Binerton, Pelham Gardens opened but not required. The initial reconnaissance made at the scene of damage by the Rescue Service Staff Officer, Mr T. Creaner, and the co-ordinated skilled rescue work performed by the C.D. Rescue Parties with military assistance under his direction, resulted in five of the trapped persons being rescued alive."

Only one shell was aimed at Folkestone. It was probably fired from the Grosser Kurfurst Batterie at Cap Gris-Nez, where the four 305-mm (12-inch) naval guns, mounted upon 360 degree traversing rings, sat above the steep cliffs. Of course, the shell could have come from any one gun of the long-range batteries.

131

By 1943 every man in the Home Guard platoons was in full service battle-dress and possessed either a rifle or sidearm, a complete set of webbing equipment, tin helmet, respirator, anti-gas cape and goggles. In three years they had, amidst the turmoil, anxiety and uncertainty, absorbed every known detachment of the earlier Local Defence Volunteers, who had paraded on Sunday mornings in civilian clothes, their only outward sign of belonging to anything at all being the cloth armband. Above: Company Sergeant Major William W. Snook, of the 8th Cinque Ports Battalion, based at the Shellon Street Territorial Army HQ, proudly leads his platoon along the Canterbury Road.   (L. Snook)

We will probably never know, but the Grosser Kurfurst Batterie held the distinction of having the Wurzburg-Riese radar installation as a method of target identification. The remainder relied on a line-of-sight target spotting technique.

Fred and Mary Palmer, two old age pensioners living at No.49 Alexander Street, died instantly when the shell detonated as it bored down through their tiny home, taking with it Nos 47 and 51. Three rescue parties arrived within ten minutes. They were joined by British and American servicemen who were billeted nearby. It was dark and the roads were covered with bricks and tiles. Three ambulances and three or four sitting-case cars arrived soon afterwards and were parked in Denmark Street, where every house had received some sort of damage by the blast effect.

Arc lights were set up, powered by auxiliary generators. Everyone rallied to the task of searching for the occupants. Civilians and servicemen worked shoulder to shoulder clawing the rubble with their bare hands. One by one the bodies were found beneath the mass of debris. George and Mary Botting, at what was once No.47, were found beneath a wardrobe which had been smashed to smithereens. It was another hour before they located Frank and Bessie Kite, at No.51. They were rushed to hospital with severe injuries, but beside the pavement lay the bodies of 65-year-old Frederick Palmer and his 70-year-old wife, covered with blankets. By 3 o'clock 18-year-old Phyllis Squirrel had been found hurt in No.39 where blast had shattered the home and, around the corner in Joyes Road, Doris Maycock was taken to hospital with severe injuries.

★

When the 21st Army Group took over the implementation of the "Overlord" cover plan, to hoodwink the German High Command into thinking the south-east was going to be the "jump-off" point for the Normandy invasion, preparations to display troop and vehicle concentrations and movements were considerably less than discreet.

In the months before D-Day most of the troops in the south-east belonged to the 1st United States Army Group under the code-name FUSAG. By May 1944 it was the 3rd United States Army of nine divisions, together with the 1st Canadian Army of two divisions, whose locations were especially divulged to the enemy through radio signals and special agents.

Folkestone and the surrounding area saw extensive troop movements at brigade and divisional strength. Large houses in the town were taken over by various American signals units whose simulated radio traffic, easily monitored by the enemy, became an important factor in the deception. The rapid movement of units in and out of the town confused the residents, let alone the enemy. Further confusion was caused by British troops darting in and out of bombed-out houses and throwing grenades and thunder-flashes in the deserted Dover Street area. The more noise they made the better the deception. But at long last the people of the town could see, at first hand, a heartening display of strength that caused a multiplicity of rumour. It was effectively the prelude to the Second Front, and yet the citizens of Folkestone were to see more blood-shed in the coming months.

Tuesday 6th June. Shelling on "D" Day convoy off Folkestone.

Tuesday 13th June. 0040 hrs to 0548 hrs — Shelling — District affected — Warren Road level crossing — Sidney Street School — Bradstone Avenue — Athelstan Road — Payers Park — Tram Road — Bayle Parade — Inner Harbour — Cricket Ground — Claremont Road — Broadmead Road — George Lane — Burrow Road and Penfold Road (waste land) — Avereng Road — Harvey Grammar School

Explanatory Leaflet on the Home Guard

1. Object

The object of the force is to augment the forces of Great Britain by providing local defence and protection of vulnerable points and by giving timely notice of enemy movement.

2. Status

The Home Guard forms part of the Armed Forces of the Crown. The members of the forces are unpaid. They are not, however, required to give whole-time service or to live away from their homes, except when mustered by reason of an actual or apprehended invasion.

Above: members of the 8th (Cinque Ports) Battaltion, Home Guard, at their Shellon Street Depot, Folkestone, 1943.

Cricket Ground — Radnore Park Bowling Green — Alder Road — Beachborough Villas — Wear Bay Road (open land) — Old Harvey Grammar School (Foord Road) — Burrow Road — Foreshore. St Eanswythe Mission Hall demolished, badly damaged were George Spurgeon School, Radnor Park Bowls Pavilion, 2 shops, 2 houses, Wesleyan Church. Slightly damaged were Central Cinema, Clinic, 20 shops, 1,010 houses. Casualties 6 male injured (3 military), 4 female injured.

This was the heaviest shell bombardment aimed at Folkestone, lasting five hours, during which 42 shells fell on or near to the Borough. It was to many Folkestonians the worst night of the whole war. Coastguards reported that enemy guns had opened fire at half an hour after midnight and the shell warning was given immediately. Within the first hour eight shells fell in the sea by the foreshore sending up huge plumes of spray. The Report Control Centre received so many telephone calls from the Royal Navy, fire guards, wardens, Home Guard and various sentries, that the lines of communication became jammed. The remaining shells which actually reached the town fell in the next ninety minutes. The German radar, used for target prediction, gave the elevation correction so that the next shell fired hit the already damaged George Spurgeon School in Sidney Street. When the police and rescue parties arrived they saw bottles of preserved snakes and lizards strewn over the playground. Then another shell exploded on the Warren Road level crossing causing window and slate damage over a very wide area. A number of shells reached Cheriton and Morehall but fortunately fell in open ground. Then Mr Pink's hardware stores in George Lane received a direct hit at the rear which almost demolished the old building and the one next door. The Radnor Bowling Pavilion collapsed from blast when one shell fell close by, and the Old Grammar School, Grace Hill, received a shell through the roof.

The constant detonations had a traumatic effect upon the townspeople who clearly heard the German long-range guns firing. They huddled in their Morrison and Anderson shelters not knowing if it was their last hour on earth. Syd Lester recalled: "Lying there listening to the shells crashing down, I thought there would be nothing left of Folkestone."

As the hours went by more shells struck built-up areas and damage was becoming more widespread. Two additional rescue parties were called from Bridge and the Binerton Rest Centre was opened. The streets became littered with debris. Tiles, slates and blocks of masonry, flung into the air, crashed through roofs and shop windows. Casualties were remarkably light despite many streets in absolute chaos. But once again the authorities would not allow Folkestone to be mentioned specifically in national newspapers. The only reference to location was "in the Dover area", and so the general public at large were led to believe that the only place to suffer shelling was Dover! Published sources on this occasion told the country that "Dover area has been shelled again". But even the town of Maidstone had received some shells; the attention to the coastal town of Folkestone was understandable, but to reach Maidstone was considered bizarre to say the least. In retrospect, however, it has been suggested the shell bombardment of both towns was to draw observers from a new deadly weapon about to be unleashed upon the Home Counties.

Immediately after 6th June 1944, when the allies landed on the Normandy beaches, the townspeople of Folkestone unquestionably felt a sense of relief — albeit premature. They eagerly sought information from BBC broadcasts and the national newspapers in the vain hope of gaining some measure of reassurance against the cessation of the terrible shelling. But when Hitler's new weapon began to appear overhead, carrying its one ton warhead and propelled by a frightening rocket motor, they were once again rendered powerless and felt a sense of humiliation.

About an hour before the shell "All Clear" was sounded in the town members of an Observer Corps post near Dymchurch heard the first raucous sounds of a pilotless aircraft approaching the coast from over the English Channel. As they telephoned to their HQ the rocket-aircraft passed their post trailing a long flame from the rocket motor.

The "Big-Gun" dual between the British and German long-range artillery was mentioned in a German radio broadcast on the evening of 4th October 1943. The German observers had noted the fire which was started in the gasworks. Widespread damage to dwellings in Clarence Street affected over 200 properties and rendered 25 people homeless, but the only casualty was 4-month-old Betty Taylor of 8 Peter Street, who was taken to hospital with shock and abrasions. Above: the abattoir in St John Street was demolished by a shell on 3rd October 1943.

As early as 1936, on the remote island of Usedom, on the Baltic, at a place called Peenemunde, a secret research establishment was built. By 1942 Werner von Braun, a leading authority on rocket propulsion, had become the director. After the devastating raid on Lubeck by Bomber Command in March 1942, Hitler ordered "attacks of a retaliatory nature" on non-military targets, thus the arguments against using indiscriminate weaponry upon civilians was regarded as insignificant.

Friday 16th June. *0126 hrs — AA Shell/V1 — District affected — Darby Place. Slight damage to 1 shop and several houses. Casualties nil.*
The V1 — Vergeltungswaffen (Weapon of Revenge) but better known to the British as the Flying Bomb, Doodlebug or Buzz-bomb, was launched from easily erected ramps in the Pas de Calais area and flew on a preset height, range and speed. However, the mass of anti-aircraft artillery was not yet in place along the south east coast when the V1s were first launched. The early morning incident on the 16th was caused by a 40-mm Bofors shell aimed at a Doodlebug exploding over Darby Place. There were to be many such incidents repeated over the next couple of months.

136

When Brigadier Burrows was looking for a suitable site for the Capel guns he reported rather ambiguously, "There are no AA guns in the Folkestone area." He seemed unaware that the 3.7-inch AA guns of the 1st Heavy AA Regt, Royal Marines, were destined for sites in and around the town boundary. D11 was sited at Hope Farm, D12 at Ridge Row Acrise, D13 was given a site below Martello Tower No.1, on the East Cliff, but did not take up that position. D14 was sited close to Martello Tower No.5 near Coolinge Lane, while D16 was positioned near Arpinge Farm. Some of these units, however, were not installed until late June 1940, others even later. In 1941 the 40mm Bofors light ack-ack guns were introduced outside the defence positions of Hawkinge and Lympne airfield.

At 1040 hrs the same day another Doodlebug, heading towards the town, was damaged by one of our patrolling Spitfires over the Channel. The fighter veered off when the AA guns opened fire for fear of being hit. A number of AA shells were seen to bounce off the V1 before one of them exploded the missile over Bolton Road. A fearful explosion resulted when the missile was already falling towards the houses. Damage was widespread because of the mid-air detonation.

Saturday 17th June. *0348 hrs — V1 — District affected — in sea off Sandgate. Damage nil. Casualties nil.*

There was only the lighted end of the missile to see when the gunners tried to aim-off at a speed of over 400 mph. The sky around the robot looked like a Guy-Fawkes gala night for about thirty seconds, then one of the exploding AA shells

137

Of the 218 shells which landed upon Folkestone and the immediate area, many were fired from the 305mm, three-gun Batterie Friedrich August, sited on a hillside near the village of La Tresorerie, near Wimille. On 17th September 1944 the battery was captured by the 8th Canadian Infantry Brigade during their assault to free Boulogne. Above: on 23rd December 1943 a shell pierced the chimney of Tolputt's Timber Yard, Tram Road. If there had been a prize for marksmanship, the German battery commander, I am sure, would have been pleased to accept the trophy.

must have upset the gyro system used in the flying bomb which immediately dived into the sea.

Saturday 24th June. 1435 hrs — Shelling — District affected — Hasborough Road — East Cliff Pavilion — East Cliff. 2 houses seriously damaged, 90 houses slightly damaged, Bruce Porter Home slightly damaged, East Cliff Pavilion slightly damaged. Casualties 7 male injured, 1 female injured.

The shell warning was given at 2.35 pm when the enemy big guns opened fire upon a convoy in the Channel. Merchant ship s.s. *Gurden Gates*, a merchant ship of 1,791 tons, was hit and casualties were brought into Folkestone Harbour by the Naval authorities. Two enemy shells exploded at the rear of the East Cliff Pavilion on the Folkestone East Battery site, and one other fell in Hasborough Road. Mrs Phylis Bellerby, 35 Wear Bay Road, was taken to hospital seriously injured and an Army vehicle removed six slightly injured military personnel from the battery site area.

The "All Clear" was sounded at 5.10 pm, and it was during this period that the rescue services were called upon to assist the Navy with casualties and distressed seamen at the harbour. A number of homeless, including merchant seamen, were accommodated in a Rest Centre over night.

All the while this was happening a number of Flying Bombs had been launched and it was an AA shell which had exploded in the roof at 35 Wear Bay Road.

Monday 26th June. *1200 hrs — AA Shell — District affected — Earls Avenue — Wear Bay Crescent. Garage partially demolished, motor car damaged, extensive damage to 1 house. Casualties nil.*

Anti-aircraft shells were becoming as dangerous as the flying bombs. One 3.7 shell took the roof off of 58 Wear Bay Crescent, while a 40-mm Bofors shell struck the garage next to 33 Earls Avenue.

Tuesday 27th June. *0010 hrs to 0230 hrs — V1s — District affected — Sandgate — Shorncliffe Barracks. Extensive damage to RASC Barracks, minor damage to houses at Sandgate. Casualties 5 military personnel slightly injured.*

There were seven flying bombs destroyed by AA fire, 3 seawards of Folkestone Harbour, 3 were exploded in mid-air over the Sandgate district and one other dived into the ground behind a barrack block at Shorncliffe.

Friday 30th June. *2213 hrs — V1 — District affected — Pond Hill Road — Shorncliffe Camp. Minor damage to military buildings, 1 school, 6 shops, 40 houses. GPO wires down. Casualties 5 military personnel slightly injured.*

The increase of the V1 menace brought one of the heaviest concentrations of AA guns into the Folkestone area, which included units of the US Army. The light anti-aircraft guns and patrolling fighters of the RAF were given selected areas within which they were to engage the flying bombs. Fighters encroaching upon an area selected for AA guns were in danger of being shot down. Some were, but the use of radar installations coupled to the gun positions enabled many flying bombs to be shot out of the sky before they reached the coast towns.

In an attempt to saturate the whole gamut of our defence structure V1s were often launched in salvos and in particularly bad weather conditions to restrict our fighter operations. The V1s came in at about 2,300 feet, rather low for the 3.7-inch guns and on the high side for the 40-mm Bofors and 20-mm cannons. But despite the enemy's tactics the Flying Bomb Counter Measures Committee in London found the answer and moved every available AA gun down to the coast.

The assembled weaponry on the south-east coast to combat the V1 menace ran into thousands. In June 1944 the AA Command's guns were largely of the successful Bofors 40-mm light anti-aircraft gun with a back-up of the 3.7-inch mobile gun capable of firing a 28 lb shell to a height of 32,000 feet. By comparison the Bofors fired clips of five, 2-lb shells to a maximum height of 12,000 feet and could get off 120 shells in one minute. The Bofors had one problem,

Inspecting the damage in George Lane soon after the town's heaviest shell bombardment on 13th June 1944. The Central Cinema entrance is on the extreme right of the picture and Mr Pink's Stores is in the centre. 88-year-old Mr Pink was the oldest shopkeeper in the town and his shell-scarred shop was looted by people who took flags and bunting on display for the King's visit in October.

One frightening aspect of shelling was the peculiarity of hearing the explosion of the shell before hearing its arrival. The opposite of a bomb. Here, in St Winifred Road, Cheriton, Frank and Doris Bills were suddenly buried beneath the wreckage of their home in the early hours of 20th January 1944. The houses were rebuilt in exactly the same style.

however, it was necessary to make a direct hit before the shell would explode. Many of them just bounced off the V1!

Ack-ack performance was improved when the new radar equipment arrived, but the biggest advance in gun technology was the arrival of the proximity fuse. Originally a British invention, it was code-named "Bonzo", and changed the whole concept of anti-aircraft accuracy. One American gunner explained: "We soon reached the stage where our 90-mm guns would only fire one shell to hit one Doodlebug."

The "Bonzo" VT (variable time) proximity fuse was activated by changes in the magnetic field when within sixty feet of the target. The sensitive fuse could explode the shell near a flock of birds or anything else within its range, but its most unfortunate characteristic was the failure of the self-destructing safety mechanism. When this happened they usually penetrated houses and caused considerable damage.

The final acquisition in weaponry was the rocket-firing "Z" batteries which were capable of firing a whole barrage of 3-inch rockets into the path of a V1 with ultimate accuracy.

The largest number of V1s destroyed met their end in the sea off Folkestone, either victims of the fighter patrols or the guns. Six hundred and two were destroyed this way and another twenty-six were blown up over the town.

Saturday 1st July. Time unknown — AA Shell — District affected — Connaught Road. Damage slight. Casualties nil.

An AA shell fired at a V1 exploded in the rear garden of 5 Connaught Road.

Monday 3rd July. 1530 hrs — V1 — District affected — Bridge Street. 9 houses demolished, 1 licenced house demolished, 18 houses partially demolished, 2 licenced houses partially demolished, 2 shops and 42 houses badly damaged, 800 houses and 40 shops slightly damaged. Casualties 1 male killed, 2 female killed, 16 male injured, 11 children injured.

This particular incident, the result of a direct hit on a V1 by an AA shell, was one of the more serious in the town and involved over 900 dwellings. The flying bomb fell on Bridge Street, near the Canterbury Road junction causing over 60 casualties.

It was classed as a major incident when nine houses and the Wheatsheaf Inn just disappeared from the face of the earth. James R. Burville, licencee of the Wheatsheaf and a sergeant in the Home Guard, was killed instantly, as were Alice Lawson and Esther Murton, living at 16 Bridge Street. Rescue Services included seven units from Folkestone, four military, two naval and one from Hythe. Among those attending the utter devastation were military personnel of the Canadian and American forces.

Within just a few seconds over 100 people had been rendered homeless, many of whom were taken to Rest Centres by an East Kent bus. They were to remain there for over thirty-six hours.

141

When a V1 fell on Bridge Street on 3rd July 1944, causing over sixty casualties, it was classed as a major incident. The Wheatsheaf public house just disappeared and the licencee, James Burville, a sergeant in the Home Guard, was killed instantly.

Miss Ellen Wilkinson (Parliamentary Secretary to Ministry of Home Security) with Mr E. Heywood with walking stick (Folkestone Town Clerk) and Chief Inspector R.J. Butcher (ARP Sub-Controller) visit men assigned to clearance work in South Street, in 1944.

This remarkable photograph shows a V1 (Doodlebug) being shot down over Folkestone in the last stages of the Flying Bomb onslaught in August 1944. The picture was taken by a 'Daily Express' newspaper correspondent from a window in Cheriton Road, the office of Joe Chandler, a taxi proprietor who drove the journalists around the south east coastal towns. Signed and dated, the picture was given to Joe Chandler as a token of thanks.

Richard Butcher, the ARP Sub-Controller, wrote in his report: "Attention must be drawn to the superlative assistance given, both during the incident and subsequently, by the British and Canadian military authorities, and by the Divisional Officer of the NFS. Officers, NCOs and men attended in force, and vehicles of all types were provided for the clearance of furniture and debris."

The final paragraph reads: "Once again I have nothing but praise for all members of the Folkestone Civil Defence, their efficiency and application to their jobs left nothing to be desired."

Police War Reserve Constable F. Stockham recalls: "People out shopping were becoming complacent. When they heard a Doodlebug overhead they used to stop and listen. A few sought shelter but others seemed to ignore the falling shrapnel. When the incident happened in Bridge Street and the Wheatsheaf pub was demolished, I found a large piece of the V1 and, because it had markings and lettering on it, I stood it up against the wall of the 'Two Bells'."

He remembered another occasion: "I was on duty at the police box outside the Central Station when a Doodlebug came over the town. Suddenly there was a huge explosion and the Doodlebug had disappeared. Bits and pieces fell in the playing fields at Canterbury Road. I phoned Inspector Butcher, who told me to

"Sylvia"

Folkestone's own "Forces Sweatheart", Daisy Solly, began her singing career at the tender age of fifteen when, for a dare, she entered a Sunday evening "Talent Night" at The Leas Cliff Hall, in June 1941. During her short career as principal vocalist she entertained thousands of servicemen, increased her repertoire and encompassed the whole gammut of the musical world. With expert tuition in stage presence, diction and breathing, she increased her confidence and went on to receive tremendous ovations. Letters of appreciation and of gratitude arrived at The Leas in their hundreds from all corners of the world. In July 1944, as the V1 menace began, "Sylvia", with Ivy Read, leader of the Hallmarks Dance Band, celebrated three years together on the stage. During the performance she sang the 1,500th request — "When We're Together Again", a song composed by Ivy Read.   (D. Evans)

go up there and stop people carrying away any souvenirs. When I arrived someone told me a boy from Grove Road had retrieved a large chunk measuring about three feet square. I eventually found the boy's mother and informed her that we were instructed to collect the remains of the missile, especially the pieces which displayed any form of stencilled lettering. Between us we managed to persuade the youngster to give up his prized possession. It was on display in the garden shed and he was charging one penny to view!"

The War Reserve Constables did fire-watching duties like the ARP or anyone else, and used the building in Shorncliffe Road, now the Police Station. Six of them used to perform one night each week on a rota basis.

"On one occasion," Stockham remembered: "I was on the Park beat, near the Victoria Hospital and near to the Golf Links, where the present Sports Centre is now. There were three or four Bofors anti-aircraft guns on the links and one of them was beside the club house in a sandbagged emplacement. Visibility was almost non-existent and there was a lot of fog around. We heard a Doodlebug going over — one of many, and saw it through a gap in the low cloud. A Lieutenant shouted a couple of commands and the gun was soon firing in the direction of the fast disappearing V1. But they were unable to see it clearly for they relied on visual contact only. But not the Americans on the Leas. The used to fire about half a dozen shells and get very close to the target with the fifth or sixth shell actually hitting the missile. They were spot on. Eventually they only needed to fire one shell to hit one V1!"

Tuesday 18th July. 1115 hrs — AA Shell — District affected — 10 Cherry Garden Avenue. Damage to roof. Casualties nil.

Wednesday 19th July. 0304 hrs — V1 — District affected — in sea at Sandgate. Blast damage only. Casualties nil.

Thursday 20th July. 1030 hrs — AA Shell — District affected — Wilberforce Road, Sandate. Slight damage. Casualties nil.
An unexploded AA shell fell through the roof of 15 Wilberforce Road, and smashed a dressing table in a bedroom.

Friday 21st July. 1115 hrs — Shell — District affected — open land near Wear Bay Road. Minor damage. Casualties nil.
This was a mystery shell which caused slight damage to three houses in the area. The official report states: "The shell was not from an AA battery, and no evidence has been obtained as to its origin."
At 1205 hrs a flying bomb struck the cliff face in the Warren. Visibility was poor and an eyewitness account suggests the motor just cut out, causing the missile to dive to the ground.

Saturday 22nd July. 1055 hrs — AA Shell — District affected — Sandgate Road. Extensive damage. Casualties nil.
A 40-mm shell exploded after passing through the roof of 168 Sandgate Road. It blew out most of the upstairs bedroom furniture.

Sunday 23rd July. 0950 hrs — AA Shell — District affected — Tile Kiln Lane. Slight damage to GPO wires. Casualties nil.

1510 hrs — AA Shell — District affected — 12 Audley Road. Slight damage to house. Casualties nil.

The Hallmarks Dance Band, leader Ivy Read, played to tea-dance audiences throughout the war years at The Leas Cliff Hall. Left to right: Alf Swain, Bert "Pip" Piper, Ivy Read and Kent Stace Paine.   ("Sylvia")

The Stan Osborne Dance Band from Brighton often played at The Leas Cliff Hall during the last war. The Leas' resident vocalist, "Sylvia", sang with most bands and orchestras.
                                                          ("Sylvia")

Photographed on the veranda of the bowls pavilion at the Cheriton Road sports ground in July 1941, ambulance drivers and nurses of the Folkestone ARP/FAP relax in the summer sunshine.

Wednesday 26th July. *0120 hrs — AA Shell — District affected — 66 Collinge Road. Slight damage to house. Casualties nil.*

1310 hrs — V1 — District affected — Sandgate. Blast damage to houses. Casualties nil.

Thursday 27th July. *1920 hrs — AA Shell — District affected — western end of Southern Railway viaduct. Slight damage. Casualties nil.*

2245 hrs — V1 — District affected — Shorncliffe Road. 2 houses demolished, 2 houses partially demolished, 150 houses minor damage, 4 shops minor damage. Casualties 2 male injured, 7 female injured.

Shortly before eleven o'clock a number of flying bombs were observed coming over the Channel at varying heights and speeds. Fighter patrols out over the sea were latching on to them before the coast was reached and AA fire became a danger. But one of the fighters was pursuing his target beyond the recognised limit. The guns fired predictably when the target became "In Range", but the fighter held on, giving small bursts of cannon fire while shells burst all around him. Within a mile of the Leas the V1 began to lose height, and roaring over the roof tops eventually crashed on "Feltonfleet School", Shorncliffe Road, near the junction with Earls Avenue. Among properties seriously damaged by the explosion were Athelstan School and the Grange, formerly used by the Kent Education Committee as a junior school.

The last Flying Bomb to fall on Folkestone fell on 31st August 1944, demolishing seven houses at the junction of Brockman Road and Coolinge Road and damaging another 600 in the area.

Feltonfleet School, evacuated since 1940, was being used as a store for furniture from bombed properties. It was levelled to the ground and all the furniture was destroyed. Blast damage all but destroyed Nos 42, 44, 46 and 48 Shorncliffe Road, and among those injured were the acting Town Sergeant and his wife, who were rendered homeless and taken to a rest centre for the night.

Saturday 29th July. *1835 hrs — V1 — District affected — in air over Sandgate. Slight blast damage. Casualties nil.*
23.30 hrs — V1 — District affected — north of Biggins Wood. Minor damage in Cheriton. Casualties nil.
Another fighter refused to veer away from the AA zone and was still firing at the flying bomb as it flew over the town. People stood and watched the missile. Suddenly the engine stopped and the flying bomb dived into the foot of the North Downs where it exploded.

Sunday 30th July. *2344 hrs — V1 — District affected — in sea off Folkestone (by AA fire). Damage nil. Casualties nil.*

Thursday 3rd August. *0041 to 2329 hrs — AA Shell and V1s. District affected — Cheriton area. Casualties 1 male killed.*
War Diary records for the county state that 18 V1s were brought down in the sea before reaching the coast — 11 as a result of AA fire and 4 shot down by fighters. A rogue AA shell fell on 6 Richmond Street, Cheriton, where 81-year-old John Beal was killed.

148

With the North Downs as a back-drop the parade assembles on the Cheriton Sports Ground to await the arrival of Their Majestys King George VI and Queen Elizabeth on 18th October 1944. The Regimental Band of the Middlesex Regiment prepares to play the National Anthem.

Friday 4th August. *0119 to 2014 hrs — V1s — District affected — Sandgate. 60 houses damaged. Casualties 1 male injured.*

Spitfires and Typhoon fighters were on patrol at first light over the Channel. The concentrated AA guns were now firing a pattern barrage which accounted for 20 flying bombs which exploded in the sea. Accuracy of the fighters was enhanced by a new gun-sight, a simple device which cost no more than one shilling to produce. The fighters got 8 flying bombs, one of which exploded quite near to the Royal Kent Hotel in Sandgate High Street, causing considerable blast damage.

Saturday 5th August. *0430 to 1857 hrs — V1s — District affected — seawards of Folkestone and Sandgate. Casualties nil.*

The German Flak Regiment 155, conducting the V1 operations from their launching sites in the Pas de Calais, were experiencing some difficulties in maintaining their offensive. Most of their equipment and materials, including over 12,000 flying bombs, were dispersed in various areas throughout Northern France. Allied bombing of the railway network and launching sites disrupted the German operation and reduced the salvos fired against England. Although the scale of this bombardment was far less than predicted, (3,000 flying bombs in 24 hours) those that did arrive put fear into the hearts of people living in what was to be called "Bomb Alley". Nevertheless, the speed and height attained by the V1 was not beyond our fighter capability and our mounting success with the new promixity fuse, brought over by the American Anti-Aircraft Regiments, took an adequate toll.

149

The royal visitors were met at the Folkestone boundary by, on the left: Mr F. Heywood, Town Clerk, and Town Mayor, F.W. Castle.

Queen Elizabeth taking an interest in the Land Army contingent on the Cheriton Sports Ground, while King George VI looks on, during their visit to Folkestone on 18th October 1944.

Her Majesty Queen Elizabeth talking to members of the National Fire Service during the royal visit to Folkestone on 18th October 1944.

Sunday 6th August. *0230 to 1700 hrs — V1s — District affected — north east of Caesar's Camp. Slight damage to houses in Crete Road. Casualties nil.*

Ten flying bombs had been destroyed by AA fire the previous day and another twelve came towards Folkestone this Sunday. Nine blew up over the sea when they entered the gun sector and another three were shot down by fighters.

Monday 7th August. *0135 hrs — V1s — District affected — north east of Ross Barracks, Shorncliffe Camp. Damage over a one mile area. Casualties nil.*

Tuesday 8th August. *0610 hrs — V1s — District affected — Foreland Avenue. 2 houses demolished, 8 partially demolished. Casualties 2 male injured, 6 female injured.*

This flying bomb was damaged over the sea area and began an erratic course towards the eastern end of the town. When the motor stopped it fell like a stone towards houses in Foreland Avenue where it exploded at No.22, causing extensive damage over a wide area. Although eight people were injured there were no fatalities.

Wednesday 9th August. *0631 to 0645 hrs — V1s — District affected — Sandgate. 30 shops damaged, 200 houses damaged by blast. Casualties nil.*

An incident report states that five flying bombs were brought down within fifteen minutes by AA fire and all were approximately 100 yards from the beach at Sandgate.

151

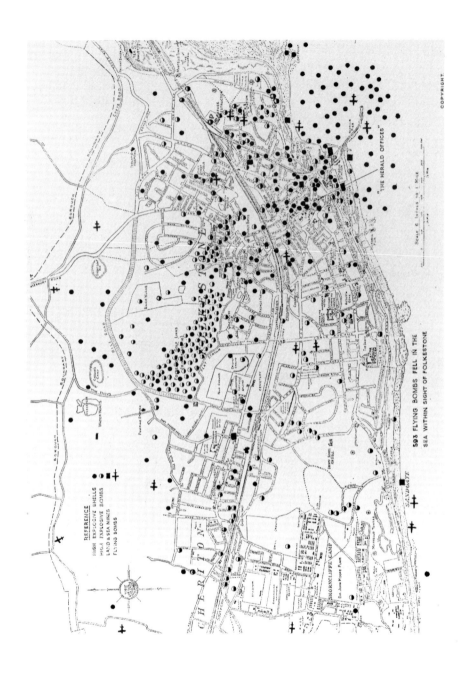

REFERENCE

HIGH EXPLOSIVE SHELLS
HIGH EXPLOSIVE BOMBS
LAND & SEA MINES
FLYING BOMBS

593 FLYING BOMBS FELL IN THE
SEA WITHIN SIGHT OF FOLKESTONE

"THE HERALD OFFICES"

SCALE 6 INCHES TO 1 MILE

COPYRIGHT

One of the Nazi flags captured by the Canadian Infantry Brigade which overrun the German long-range batteries in the Cap-Gris-Nez area in September 1944. The flag is now a prized artefact in the Folkestone Museum, having been presented to the town by the Canadian Commander.

Thursday 10th August. *0405 to 21.30 hrs — V1s — District affected — in sea. Damage nil. Casualties nil.*

Four flying bombs dived into the sea and another two were detonated by fighters.

Friday 11th August. *0721 to 1409hrs — V1s — District affected — Leas and Sandgate Road. 13 shops damaged, 30 hotels and houses damaged. Casualties nil.*

Six flying bombs were exploded in a direct line with the town. Four, exploded by the guns, appeared very low and were expected to hit tall buildings standing in their path. The blast damage was extensive although confined to roofs and windows.

Saturday 12th August. *0140 to 0615 hrs — V1s — District affected — Grimston Gardens. 3 houses demolished, 6 houses partially demolished, 20 houses extensively damaged. Casualties 1 male injured.*

Although six flying bombs were brought down over the sea one flew upside down until the motor cut. It then crashed on 21 and 23 Grimston Gardens, a large but fortunately unoccupied house, causing serious damage to the structure. Rescue units were now known as Civil Defence workers. They worked long hours clearing up the streets after a flying bomb incident and were under such pressure throughout the period of V1 attacks that other parties were sent

153

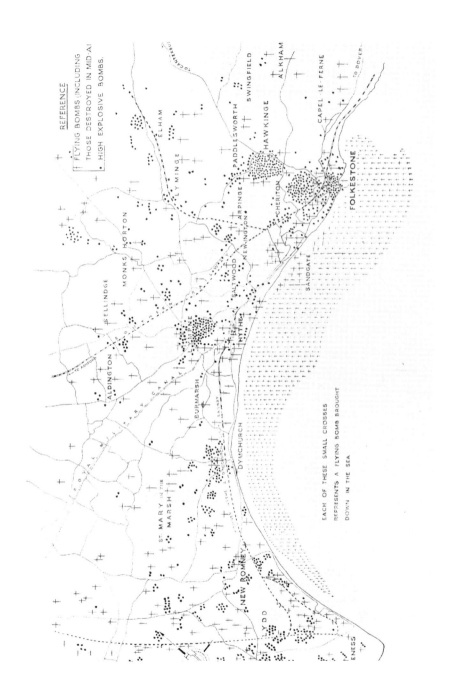

REFERENCE

FLYING BOMBS INCLUDING
THOSE DESTROYED IN MID-AIR

HIGH EXPLOSIVE BOMBS.

EACH OF THESE SMALL CROSSES
REPRESENTS A FLYING BOMB BROUGHT
DOWN IN THE SEA

154

for from other parts of the county and Sussex. Frequently the first people on the scene after an incident in a residential area were American and British gunners, whose guns had brought down the missiles. Rest centres were in constant use and during one period over 180 people were supplied with meals from mobile kitchens.

Sunday 13th August. *0110 to 0610 hrs — V1s — District affected — seaward of Folkestone. Damage nil. Casualties nil.*

Monday 14th August. *0143 to 0430 hrs — V1s — District affected — seaward of Folkestone. Damage nil. Casualties nil.*

Tuesday 15th August. *0856 to 1856 hrs — V1s — District affected — seaward of Folkestone — Sandgate. Slight damage to houses. Casualties nil.*

Wednesday 16th August. *0520 to 2120 hrs — V1s and AA Shells — District affected — Sandgate — Danton Pinch — Hawkins Road — Foord Road — Marshall Street — Hill Road. Roof damage. Casualties 1 female, 1 child.*
Over 36 flying bombs were plotted destroyed over the sea with three others having got through the fighter and gun screen unscathed to eventually blow up over Sandgate and Danton Pinch. As much damage was caused by AA shells exploding in close proximity to houses and shopping areas as that caused by the flying bombs exploding above the town. 6 Marshall Street received an AA shell where a woman and child were found suffering from shock.

Thursday 17th August. *0630 to 2041 hrs — V1s — District affected — Sandgate — Wear Bay Crescent. Damage in radius 200 yards (Sandgate) Wear Bay — 4 houses demolished, 3 houses partially demolished, 4 houses badly damaged, 1 church hall badly damaged, 5 shops badly damaged, 400 houses slightly damaged. Casualties 1 male injured, 3 female injured, 3 children injured.*
Another 29 flying bombs met their destruction out over the sea. If they had been piloted like an ordinary aeroplane they would have veered away from the formidable AA barrage which attempted to bar their progress towards London. It was inevitable that a percentage got through this barrage but our fastest fighters were waiting for them. The last line of defence was the balloon barrage around the metropolis. Folkestonians were seeing a different kind of action now. They were used to the sounds of German bombers and fighters, the special crump of exploding shells fired from over the Channel, and now the formidable barrage of anti-aircraft fire at close quarters, not to mention the distinctive sound of a flying bomb approaching the town at over 400 mph. At night it was even more spectacular. Searchlights, tracer shells and demons with fiery tails. Night-clad children sat at open windows and watched in awe and fascination during the sultry August nights. They saw a galaxy of fire crackers following these fiery tails until there was a split second when everything for

155

SUMMARY OF ENEMY ACTIONS UP TO AND INCLUDING 5th.OCTOBER 1944

```
SUMMARY OF ENEMY ACTIONS UP TO AND INCLUDING 5th.OCTOBER 1944

INCIDENTS...............164......RAIDS 102, SHELLING 36, FLY BOMBS 26.
KILLED.................123 )
INJURED...............778 } 901
BOMBS. H.E............523
BOMBS I.B............1112
SHELLS.............. 218
FLY BOMBS............ 26
FLY BOMBS............ 602......DESTROYED SEAWARDS OF FOLKESTONE
ALERTS................2914 )
CUCKOO (ALARM)........1235 }...4251
SHELLING............. 102 )
PROPERTIES BADLY DAMAGED.......14,141
SHELLING WARNING SYSTEM INTRODUCED 16th.NOVEMBER 1942
KILLED...............AIR RAIDS..88, SHELLING..32, FLY BOMBS..3
INJURED.............. -do-   460,   -do- 166,   -do- 152
```

The official "Summary of Enemy Actions" compiled by Lt Colonel Clark, Folkestone's Chief Air Raid Warden, and signed by him.

miles around was lit-up by the explosion. Such spellbound education became firmly imprinted on the children's minds, never to be erased by subsequent events in their lives.

Friday 18th August. *0006 to 0724 hrs — V1s — District affected — Sandgate in sea. Damage nil. Casualties nil.*

Before "D" Day the Royal Pavilion Hotel had, under the code-name Operation Fortitude, become H.M.S. *Allenby*. John Glover, now Marine Controller at the Rescue Co-ordination Centre, of the Halifax Search & Rescue Region, Nova Scotia, joined the Royal Navy as an ordinary seaman towards the end of 1943.

He recalls, "Under age and to compound the felony I volunteered to serve in what was then known as Combined Operations, manned by personnel drawn from the three services and the Royal Marine Commando and other oddities such as Ian Fleming's bunch of desperadoes whose vowed intention was to make themselves a nuisance in occupied territory. On the fringes of all this stood the LCIs (Landing Craft Infantry) and their crews, the Royal Navy Commando Observers who were to control off-shore Naval gunfire. The Royal Pavilion Hotel held the landing craft crews and many of the Beach Commando. They slept eight to a room and it was, by definition, a base where the Navy stored their unemployed and sometimes their unemployable.

"It was after 'D' Day when a vessel — s.s. *Fort Gloucester*, was torpedoed ten and a half miles east of Dungeness by an 'E' Boat. The vessel was moored alongside the pier and from the third floor of the Pavilion Hotel there was no sign of damage. Secured across the end of the sea wall — bows to the beach and stern to the open sea — she did not appear to be down by the stern, although we were informed the very next day that she had been hit aft near the propeller. The sea wall was placed 'out of bounds' to all ranks which precluded closer inspection.

"S.s. *Fort Gloucester*, after several days, had become part of the local scene; not forgotten but not really a source of conversation either. That is, until one pleasant summer's evening the vessel caught fire. A puzzling fire, no smoke or flame and no stampeding bodies. The NFS arrived and a pump was dropped near a concrete ramp on the landward side of the sea wall.

"There was a falling tide and the ramp was covered with a morass of marine life which, before long, blocked the intake hose of the pump. Failing to suck up water, the pump was moved by Navy muscle but, after a period of idiocy, when the pump was almost lost, the Royal Engineers were persuaded to use a bull-dozer. Eventually the fire was brought under control.

"We were unaware of the ship's cargo until two days later, which did nothing for anybody's peace of mind — we learned that we had been on a ship carrying 200,000 gallons of petrol in Jerry cans!"

Saturday 19th August. *0310 to 0600 hrs (Sunday 20th). V1s — District affected — Fishmarket. Extensive damage to Fishmarket and harbour buildings, houses and shops. Casualties 1 male injured, 5 female injured.*

Three flying bombs were sent into the sea just after three o'clock in the morning, a fraction of the total missiles launched. When townspeople were getting up from their disturbed sleep a flying bomb dived onto the Southern Railway Pier, causing widespread damage to harbour equipment and buildings. Throughout the night flying bombs had been launched in a desperate attempt to demoralise the citizens of London. But night firing results were not always clear to the German commanders whose views varied as to whether day or night firing was the most successful. It had been decided as early as July that because of the flame from the engine it gave the clearest indication of the weapon's course and therefore day launching, particularly in bad weather conditions, would be the answer. Despite the uncertainty night launches were made in

GROUP C

Air Raid Warden's Office,
Town Hall,
Folkestone.

30th December, 1938.

Dear Sir or Madam,

The Warden organisation in Folkestone is being re-arranged to conform more closely with the organisation suggested by the Home Office - please refer to A.R.P. Handbook No 8, 2nd Edition, "The Duties of Air Raid Wardens", (pages 4,5,6 and 7)

The Town has been divided into 6 GROUPS, to be known as Group H, (Harbour); Group J, (Junction); Group T, (Town); Group P, (Park); Group W, (Western); and Group C, (Cheriton). The following have been appointed Deputy Head Wardens.

H	Group	J.J.Galvin Esq., Victoria Hotel	Telephone	306411
J	Group	C.Wenham Esq., 212 Canterbury Road	"	3113
T	Group	E.A.George Esq., 76 Sandgate Road	"	3669
W	Group	A.T.Maggs Esq., 6 Earls Avenue	"	3552
P	Group	P.E.Martin Esq., (Acting Leas Hotel)	"	2225
C	Group	W.C.Piggott Esq., Enbrook Manor	"	85283

The Deputy Group Head Wardens are proceeding to find further Wardens Posts, on the basis of one post to every 500 population about 90 posts in all. As soon as this has been done, posts will be numbered and when the scheme is complete each post will be manned by 6 Wardens, (1 Senior Warden, 1 Second Warden and 4 Wardens)

A map showing the new Group boundaries is available for inspection in this office and the reference at the top of this letter indicates which group you are in.

Will you please put your Group letter and your own number on all correspondence.

Yours truly,
H.C.Green
Chief Warden.

```
┌─────────────────────────────────────┐
│                                     │
│   PUBLIC WARNING                    │
│   ..............................    │
│                                     │
│                                     │
│   Gun Practice                      │
│                                     │
│   will be carried out in the        │
│                                     │
│   Area Dover to Hastings            │
│                                     │
│   from 18th to 20th June,           │
│                                     │
│   1940 between the hours            │
│                                     │
│   10 a.m. and 10 p.m.               │
│                                     │
│                                     │
│            GEORGE FEW,              │
│                 Mayor.              │
│                                     │
│   ──────────────────                │
│   J. Lovick & Sons, Printers, High Street. │
│                                     │
└─────────────────────────────────────┘
```

defiance of an order to the contrary, largely because of the Allied advances from the Normandy Front.

Another flying bomb exploded over the harbour at 2.30 pm when it had received a direct hit by AA fire. No.17 Wear Bay Crescent lost most of its roof.

Sunday 20th August. *0600 to 1443 hrs — V1s — District affected — Sandgate. Slight damage to property. Casualties 2 female, 2 children injured.*

Twenty-three flying bombs failed to reach the coastline, five of them being shot down by patrolling Hawker Tempests, the latest RAF fighter, held back in Britain for the flying bomb offensive.

Monday 21st August. *0212 to 2054 hrs — V1s and AA Shells — District affected — East Cliff — Grimston Avenue — the Bayle. Damage to buildings caused by AA shells. Casualties nil.*

While our fighters and guns were shooting down 16 flying bombs, green coloured shell caps were falling all over the town. Some took away chimney-pots, roof tiles and bedroom windows, others failed to explode and fell through roofs into bedrooms like the one at 23A East Cliff. The 'Herald' printing office received one which brought down the ceilings and plaster. Employees, covered in a fine dust, resembled chimney-sweeps. Another shell sailed through

Martello Tower No.3 stands above Copt Point and was within the boundary of Folkestone East Battery. The concrete structure on top was a Naval Observation Post in connection with mine laying in the Dover Straits. The concrete building on the right of the tower was built in 1943 as a Battery Observation Post (BOP) for the East Cliff guns.

Councillor R.G. Wood wrote to 'The Folkestone & Hythe District Herald' on Saturday 27th June 1940: "WHO EXPECTS FOLKESTONE TO BE BOMBARDED OR INVADED?" — he went on: "The former would take months to prepare on the French coast and would have to be done secretly without the watchful eye of the RAF detecting it. What a Task! The latter would require hundreds of barges or scores of transports and a concentration of tens of thousands of men to have a chance of success." Above: an RAF reconnaisance photograph showing the concentration of invasion barges at Boulogne Harbour. German invasion barges were also massed at Calais, Dunkirk, Ostend and Zeebrugge.

All that remains of the Folkestone East (Copt Point) Battery site situated immediately behind the East Cliff Pavilion. Nearest the camera is No.1 Gun with its magazine attached, No.2 Gun position is seen beyond, where the cliff face is crumbling more than two feet each year.

windows at 25 Grimston Avenue and reappeared at 27 Grimston Avenue, taking out the window casement.

Tuesday 22nd August. *0325 to 0600 hrs. V1s — District affected — seaward of Folkestone. Damage nil. Casualties nil.*

Of the 31 flying bombs which are recorded in the vicinity during a period lasting over twenty-four hours, 22 were brought down by the AA barrage. The sky was over-cast and gave the gunners a difficult time. The United States units, however, using their radar installations, put up a formidable array of 90-mm shells on a set height and range prediction. Fighters on "Diver Patrol" were in constant danger of being shot down and tended to fly further out to sea to catch their prey long before they arrived in the danger area. ("Diver" was the RAF code-name for flying bomb.)

In the early hours of Wednesday 23rd, a fighter managed to see a flying bomb through a break in the cloud base and quickly shot it down.

Thursday 24th August. *0240 to 2115 hrs — V1s — District affected — seawards of Folkestone. Damage nil. Casualties nil.*

To assist with the sudden increase of flying bombs launched, a couple of naval boats, bristling with pom-poms, cannons and the latest anti-aircraft rocket projectiles, were stationed off the harbour. They accounted for two of the 39 destroyed this day. One AA shell blew out the interior of a room at 27 Manor Road.

On 8th September 1940, the two 9.2-inch railway guns of the 4th Super-Heavy Railway Battery, RA, moved to their respective positions at Hythe and Folkestone. The "Right Section" gun was named "S.M. Cleeve", and was positioned on the Hythe sidings. The "Left Section" gun called "E.E. Gee" went into the railway sidings at Folkestone East (Junction) Station, just west of the short tunnel leading to the coastal line to Dover. The Folkestone gun fired its first round on 18th October 1940, when the 86 ton gun jumped off the rails. The photograph was taken between Ashford and Hythe.   ('Kent Messenger')

Friday 25th August. *0704 — V1s — District affected — seaward of Folkestone. Damage nil. Casualties nil.*
Only one flying bomb recorded shot down by AA fire.

Sunday 27th August. *0630 to 0652 hrs — V1s — District affected — seaward of Folkestone. Damage nil. Casualties nil.*
Nine flying bombs are recorded as shot down in sea by AA, and one telegraph pole outside "Skerryvore", The Undercliffe!

Monday 28th August. *1420 to 1926 hrs — V1s — District affected — seawards of Folkestone. Damage nil. Casualties nil.*
Sea-mist and low cloud disrupted the gunners accuracy and the radar seemed to go "haywire" (as one American described the day's events). Even so the gunners managed to shoot down 36 before they reached the coast.

Tuesday 29th August. *1730 to 2332 hrs — V1s and AA Shells — District affected — Bradstone Road. Slight damage. Casualties 1 male injured, 1 female injured.*
The first flying bomb heading towards Folkestone was intercepted by a fighter. It was in full view of the gunners, anxious to open fire as it hurtled

towards their sector. Dozens of binoculars were trained on the scene as the Tempest fired a series of short bursts. But the flying bomb continued on its course. And so did the Tempest. It was still firing its cannons when both flying bomb and fighter entered the gun-belt. 90-mm shells began to explode in front of the missile. The Tempest pilot seemed oblivious of the danger. Then the flying bomb disappeared in a huge explosion. The pilot was unable to avoid it and flew through the detonating debris. Everyone expected to see the fighter dive into the sea. Instead, it appeared from out of this powerful, black cloud of destructive explosive, upside down but still flying. It righted itself over the town and with smoke trailing from the engine made a reasonable landing at RAF Hawkinge.

Of the 34 flying bombs shot down near the town this day a couple of them carried a quantity of leaflets. The beach area below the Leas Cliff Hall was littered with them. The leaflets were similar to those dropped on Germany by Bomber Command, and also appeared in other places in Kent and Sussex. There was an immediate security clamp-down. Police, troops and Civil Defence Units were told to collect them and hand them to the Military authorities.

One AA shell went through the roof of No.1 Bradstone Road, injuring the occupants.

Wednesday 30th August. *0008 to 1310 hrs — V1s — District affected — Danton Pinch. Damage to farm buildings and houses. Casualties nil.*

Although 10 flying bombs were shot down by the guns one of them continued on its course until it blew up in mid-air close to Danton Farm. The farm, northwest of Cheriton, was always beneath one invisible track along which the missiles flew towards their target — London. There were occasional deviations from that path when a flying bomb had been damaged in flight or it had corrected its own line of flight when upset by exploding shells. An example of this is recalled by Constable Stockham:

"One Sunday afternoon at Sandgate, I was on duty in the area known as the Riviera. People were walking around when a Doodlebug came over the sea very low. Then it started to change course. It went right then left, then did a couple of loops and then began to circle. The engine sounded intermittent. It then gave a burst of speed, then failed and picked up again. Obviously something was at fault. Shells were exploding all round it. One or two women were walking along the Riviera and I told them to take cover in case the thing exploded overhead. They started to run, one this way, one the other way. I shouted to them to 'STOP!'. They looked at me as if I was the last human on earth. I said: 'Get under cover!' They both looked at me and one of them said: 'What for?'. I replied: 'Well — it's no good running all over the place — get alongside the wall.' I had no sooner said that when the V1 turned out to sea with its engine pulsating until it was out of sight. It must have reached France. The two women just stood there and laughed at me."

The organisation of the new volunteer Auxiliary Fire Service in April 1938, quickly outnumbered the regulars when, following the Munich crisis, thousands of men and women signed up. The severe air raids on London and the Home Counties showed the weaknesses of the hotch-potch Fire Service in which there were no two alike in either equipment or skills. At a conference to discuss the future of the Fire Service in war, held on 28th April 1941, the then Home Secretary (Mr Herbert Morrison) announced his decision to nationalise the Service. The plan was put to Parliament on 13th May, and a week later the Fire Service (Emergency Provisions) Bill 1941, became law. The independent fire authorities were absorbed into the National Fire Service on 18th August 1941.

Bombs and incendiaries were scattered over a wide area on Sunday 17th January 1943. The bombs were of the delayed-action type and two fell in Lennard Road which exploded on the following day. Above: Nos 1 and 2 Lennard Road collapsed in a heap of rubble.

164

Thursday 31st August. *0959 to 1742 hrs — V1s — District affected — Brockman Road — Claremont Road — Cambridge Gardens — Broadmead Road — Guildhall Street — Coolinge Road. 4 houses demolished, 4 houses partially demolished, 6 houses extensively damaged, 400 houses slightly damaged. Labour Exchange slightly damaged. Casualties 19 male injured, 31 female injured, 5 children injured.*

Of the 26 flying bombs which actually fell on Folkestone, the one which exploded on houses almost opposite the bottom of Claremont Road — in Brockman Road, probably caused the greatest damage of any incident in the town. It was truly catastrophic. Rows of houses suffered tremendous blast damage. Thousands of windows shattered and complete roofs of tiles were ripped off rafters as if by an unseen hand. While the Civil Defence Units clambered over huge mounds of bricks, tiles and masonry, to reach those people trapped beneath, more flying bombs hurtled over the town. Nineteen were blown up by accurate AA fire and a further three were shot down by fighters. Perhaps the most remarkable aspect was that there were no fatalities that day. There were over 100 bathers on the East Cliff Sands when one flying bomb exploded almost over them, but no one was hurt.

This particular phase of German aggression was drawing to a close. The Allied armies spearhead consisting of the British 21st Army Group were, on 26th August, just north of Abbeville, thus driving the Flak Regiment 155 W from their positions between Dieppe and Boulogne. Stores and equipment were destroyed while the last remaining missiles were prepared for firing. In the following month the German long-range guns were also under siege, but not before they too made every effort to discharge as many shells as they could. They managed to pound the borough with sixty-four shells in the month of September.

Friday 1st September. *0014 hrs to 0240 hrs — Shelling and V1s — District affected — the Stade — Bellevue Street — Brickfields — Park Farm — foreshore at East Cliff — Margaret Street — Bradstone Avenue — Caesar's Camp. Fire Station (Dover Road) extensively damaged, 2 houses partially demolished, 14 houses slightly damaged, gasometer slightly damaged. Casualties 3 male injured, 7 female injured.*

Chief Inspector Butcher began his report for September: "Gentlemen, Folkestone, during the month of September 1944, endured with its neighbouring coastal towns, the most intensive period of cross-Channel shelling since the first enemy shells fired at this country landed on the morning of 12th August 1940. Having regard to the many exceptional features of the various incidents, and the large scale of reinforcements it became necessary to engage, I propose to render this report at some length, and under particular headings."

Butcher included in the four-page report most of the statistical details relating to the 64 shells which fell on the borough, but somehow forgot to mention the three flying bombs (recorded elsewhere). Of the eight shells that fell on the town this Friday, that which exploded on Margaret Street was the most severe.

Fire-fighting in Folkestone was not a major hazard although incendiaries and oil-pots, scattered over a wide area, were particularly frustrating. High explosive shells, however, did not usually cause serious outbreaks of fire. Nevertheless, the fire crews were often in the forefront of rescue work and in repairing damaged property. The courage of the fire-fighter, in whatever circumstances, was never in question and many Folkestone firemen were injured whilst protecting life and property.

The first of three flying bombs launched just after midnight demolished a house near the Alkham Valley crossroads. When the other two arrived one was picked-off by a night fighter and the other by concentrated AA fire.

Mrs Anita Williams was a heroine in the night's proceedings. Public recognition of her services was made by order of the King in the 'London Gazette': "During the shelling bombardment of 1st Sept: 1944, (at night) two houses in the fishmarket were demolished by a direct hit. Within a matter of a minute or two Mrs Williams, a 52-year-old ARP warden, a widow with two sons serving overseas, arrived on the scene wearing just an overcoat over her nightdress. She clambered over wreckage to find the occupants of the wrecked homes and, although bleeding from a nasty leg wound, she insisted on remaining with people she found in a shelter. She remained on duty, reassuring the occupants throughout the bombardment; her calmness and courage was an example to all."

Saturday 2nd September. 0130 hrs — Shelling — District affected — Hill Road — Canterbury Road — Folkestone Road — Bowles-Well Gardens. 1 house demolished, 2 houses seriously damaged, 50 houses slightly damaged. Casualties 1 male injured, 4 female injured.

Three shells fell almost in a straight line, one of them exploding on 38 Hill Road. But no one could offer an explanation for the 20-mm cannon shell that bored its way through the roof of 3 The Durlocks.

Sunday 10th September. 1028 hrs — Shelling — District affected — Dudley Road — on foreshore. 3 houses demolished, 20 houses seriously damaged, 50 houses slightly damaged. Casualties 2 female killed, 5 male injured, 5 female injured, 3 children injured.

A couple of "ranging shells" fell in the sea just before 10.30 am, but the following salvo accurately plastered Dudley Road. Folkestone West Battery had a narrow escape because the shells fell only one hundred yards away.

Damage was widespread and Sunday lunch was provided by the mobile kitchen units for both the Civil Defence personnel and the residents. Eighty-year-old Mrs Margaret Mockett was found beneath her wrecked home at 38 Dudley Road, severely injured. Unfortunately she died of her wounds at the Royal Victoria Hospital two days later. Her daughter, 47-year-old Daisy Mockett, was later found dead under the debris. A large number of people were made homeless and taken to the Pelham Gardens Rest Centre, but later that week some were sent to Herne Bay, Hythe and Saltwood.

Monday 11th September. 0225 hrs — Shelling — District affected — field adjacent to Cherry Garden Avenue. Casualties 24 sheep.

Wednesday 13th September. 1110 hrs to 1645 hrs — Shelling — District affected — Dolphins Road — Cooks Orchard — Tile Kiln Lane — Waterworks Hill — Rita Place — Caesar's Camp — Shaftesbury Avenue. 4 houses demolished, 4 houses partially demolished, 130 houses slightly damaged. Casualties 1 female killed, 5 male injured, 15 female injured, 4 children injured.

The German long-range guns, despite their almost continuous pounding by Bomber Command and the 8th USAAF, during both day and night operations, still managed to fire their salvos each day. It was the hour before mid-day when the greenhouses near Tile Kiln Lane were wrecked completely by one shell. Another salvo reached Caesar's Camp, just short of Hawkinge airfield.

At a quarter to five another salvo reached the town. Rescue services were already at the New Era Laundry in Shaftesbury Avenue, where a number of female employees were receiving first aid to their cuts and bruises. Rescuers looked up from their labours when they heard the CRUMP! CRUMP! of two more shells. Black smoke spiralled above a residential area. Divisional Officer Woods of the NFS moved his standby team of sixteen men with their equipment from their posts to Dolphins Road and Rita Place. It was at 13 Rita Place where 66-year-old Charlotte Simpson was discovered beneath the wreckage of her home. Within twenty-four hours there were more deaths in the town.

Thursday 14th September. 1200 hrs to 2120 hrs — Shelling — District affected — Radnor Park Gardens — Radnor Park Crescent — Hill Road — outer harbour — open ground Cheriton — Caesar's Camp — Golf Links — Charlotte Street — Coolinge Lane — Danton Pinch — Alkham Crossroads — East Cliff Sands — Royal Victoria Hospital — Fosters Laundry — Cherry Garden Lane — Castle Hill —

While the larger ENSA shows were usually booked for the Pavilion Theatre, The Leas entertainments centred on individual variety acts and the many dance bands and orchestras which toured seaside towns. Among them were dance bands from the Royal Air Force and Army. ("Sylvia")

Morehall open ground. 7 houses demolished, 5 houses partially demolished, 100 houses badly damaged, 600 houses slightly damaged. Casualties 1 male killed, 4 female killed, 1 child killed, 10 male injured, 26 female injured, 2 children injured.

The Canadian First Army were advancing towards Calais and the German long-range guns were strongly defended in their fortified positions.

Soon to be overwhelmed by the Canadians, the German gunners, however, were obstinate in the face of adversity. With over a thousand shells to each gun still waiting in the massive concrete bunkers there was to be no respite for the British coastal towns.

Shelling started about midday and went on until after dusk. The greatest number of casualties occurred on this day when over 20 shells fell in the Folkestone area.

The first shell fell in Radnor Park Crescent, demolishing a house where a number of ENSA artists were staying with Mr and Mrs Kellett, who were both seriously injured. Two members of the ENSA party were slightly injured.

Shells fell in salvos of four at intervals, some of them fortunately exploding in open ground between the town and the Downs. During the afternoon the Royal Victoria Hospital was damaged when a house in nearby Radnor Park Gardens was hit, leaving three dwellings beyond repair. But shortly before five o'clock a shell caused the deaths of two women in Charlotte Street, Mrs Martha Kendall at No.13 and Mrs Amelia Packer living next door at No.15. The shelling continued in the evening and at 9.37 pm the western end of the Royal Victoria Hospital received a direct hit. In the hospital at the time were over 60 patients, including a number of people who had earlier that day been injured by the bombardment. Fortunately the evening staff had moved all the patients into the shelters provided in the sun-basement and none were hurt. However, in the nurses' sitting room, Miss Vivienne Ibbet, aged twenty-two, was killed, and also Miss Florence Haswell, a linen maid who was in the linen room. Perhaps the most tragic death was that of 8-week-old Vivienne Elliott, asleep in her cot.

Outside the hospital and only a short distance away, 57-year-old Sergeant Bush, who was returning to his home at Marten Road after Home Guard duties, was struck by many shell splinters which killed him instantly. The hospital almoner, Mrs Setterfield, had left the nurses' sitting room to post a letter. She was thrown through a glass partition when the shell struck and received serious injuries. Others injured were nurses Joyce Venetti, Joy Holter, Kathleen Brooker, Marjorie Summer, and Mrs Cochrane.

Damage to the hospital structure meant the immediate removal of patients. A fleet of ambulances and cars soon evacuated them to other hospitals, including the Emergency Military Hospital of the RAMC, at the Hotel Metropole, where Colonel Love organised teams of nursing orderlies. Some hospital staff, however, remained at the Royal Vic, as it has always been called, to clear up the wreckage of the cubicle wards and the nurses' home. During the weekend RAF Typhoon fighter-bombers made a rocket attack on the powerful lighthouse between Boulogne and Calais, a famous landmark used by the Germans as an observation post for the long-range guns.

Friday 15th September. *1737 hrs to 2258 hrs — Shelling — District affected — in sea — East Cliff Sands — Canterbury Road — Downs Road — Walton Gardens. 5 houses partially demolished, 6 houses badly damaged, 50 houses slightly damaged, 8 shops damaged, 1 public house damaged. Casualties 2 male killed, 1 male injured, 5 female injured.*

It was just after 5.30 pm when the bombardment was renewed from the previous day's events. Several salvos fell in the sea close to the East Cliff Sands. The height and range were adjusted which brought the next salvo onto the Canterbury Road and Black Bull Road area, one shell exploding only a few yards away from St Saviour's Church, causing tremendous damage and killing an RAF airman who was walking by the church. Another shell exploded in the front garden of 29 Walton Gardens, causing the death of Police Sergeant William George Dickinson. Both his wife and daughter were seriously injured.

An estate on the hillside suffered major damage and casualties. PC Crane was sent to the area to patrol the scene and keep away looters. He recalled: "It did not please me to hear the shelling warning and within seconds I was alone, as everyone had wisely taken precautions and gone into their shelters. But this was the time when insecure property was most vulnerable to the light-fingered

The American crew of a 90mm AA gun — one of four sited beside the Hotel Imperial, Hythe, brought down to the coastal areas to implement the defence barrage against the "Doodlebug" in 1944.   (J. Jahnke)

fraternity. I sat on a low garden wall and lit a cigarette. Then a shell burst on open ground higher up the hill. I convinced myself that shells did not fall in the same place twice. My feelings of isolation were broken when I saw my patrol sergeant pushing his cycle up the hill towards me. DAMN! — he's caught me smoking and I hastily dropped my cigarette."

PC Crane remembers vividly the incident which killed Police Sergeant Dickinson.

"The police were still working a twelve-hour day but were allowed one day off from duty each week from midnight to midnight. Shells were falling all over the town on this particular night. My wife and two daughters, together with a neighbour and her son, took cover in the Morrison shelter in our lounge. I was with them, fervently hoping the "All Clear" would sound before I went on duty at midnight. Then we were shaken by a terrific crunch. The lights went out and all the small, loose articles were suddenly sucked up the chimney.

"That shell burst proved to be a tragedy for my patrol sergeant and his family. He, like me, was waiting to go on duty at midnight. He heard the shell burst and had gone out to see where it had exploded. He walked into the blast of the second shell. His poor wife, who already suffered badly from nerves, remembered her husband turned towards the house with his face blown away. He collapsed and died almost immediately."

Saturday 23rd September. *1415 hrs — Shelling — District affected — Radnor Bridge Road — 2 houses badly damaged, 100 houses slight damage. Casualties 1 male killed, 1 male injured, 5 female injured.*

Just one shell was fired at Folkestone in the early afternoon. Perhaps the rocket attack on the German observation post had upset their aim. But whatever the reason that one shell must have had a name written upon its casing. Albert John Relen, a well-known Folkestone licensee, was killed outright when the shell detonated close to his garden at 11 Radnor Bridge Road. Mrs Relen was seriously injured and at one time it was feared she might lose her sight. Albert had been a resident of the town since 1934 and had been the proprietor of the Royal George Hotel, Beach Street. The family had been bombed out no fewer than nine times!

Monday 25th September. *1106 hrs to 1626 hrs — Shelling — District affected — the Leas — Harvey Grammar School — Beachborough Villas — the beach. Extensive damage to Grammar School, "Castlehaven" Hotel badly damaged, 1 house badly damaged, 100 houses slightly damaged. Casualties 4 male injured, 6 female injured.*

Folkestone was under shellfire for the last time which began just one hour before midday. Two shells exploded in the Morehall area, one hitting the Harvey Grammar School and the other just yards away in the rear garden of a house in Beachborough Road. Another two shells in the salvo of four reached open ground beyond Cheriton. The next salvo, and the last shells to be fired at the town, was almost, or so it seemed, to be fired in desperation.

Two shells plopped into the sea about a thousand yards from the seashore, the next exploded on the beach below the Leas sending up tons of pebbles. But the last shell blew out the top of Castlehaven Hotel, near the Leas Cliff Hall. Most of the guests were downstairs at the time and escaped injury. Among those staying there were members of an ENSA party booked to appear at the Pleasure Gardens Theatre that week. Many of them lost their personal belongings when the bedrooms collapsed in a heap. Because of the unpredictable state of the shelling so far experienced coupled with their loss of property the artistes returned to London on the next available train. They were quite unaware that the shell which destroyed their belongings was the last to reach Folkestone.

Although shells continued to fall on Dover the following day, Folkestone's ordeal was over. The Canadian First Army had overrun the gun positions.

During the shelling ordeal the life of the town was seriously disrupted. Cinemas and theatres and many other places of entertainment were either closed during the shell warning period, or were shut for longer periods, some remaining closed for weeks. Deep shell craters appeared all over the town. Some shells exploded in the air which caused streets to become more or less deserted. Some shops closed while others remained open. Bus services were curtailed and some trains stopped outside the town until the "All Clear" had been sounded.

In an attempt to saturate our defence structure the V1s were often launched in salvos but, despite the enemy's tactics, the Flying Bomb Counter Measures Committee in London found the answer and moved not only light ack-ack guns in to the area, but also the rocket-firing "Z" batteries which were capable of releasing a whole barrage of 3-inch rockets into the path of the V1s with dire results.

It was on Saturday 30th September that several cars with a public address system broadcast a message to the townspeople from street to street, announcing that at last, after more than four years, the menace of the German long-range guns was finally over. "A special announcement for the citizens of Folkestone. His worship the Mayor (Alderman A. Castle) has received official information from SHAEF that all of the long-range guns on the other side of the Channel have been captured."

Within minutes bedroom windows which had not been disturbed for years gradually opened. Here and there pieces of coloured bunting began to appear, draped over windowsills and, above the Town Hall, a Union Jack fluttered with the Cross of St George hoisted above the Parish Church on the Bayle.

During a celebration dance held at the Leas Cliff Hall the following weekend a message of grateful thanks was sent to General Crerar, commanding the Canadian Forces of the British Liberation Army, which read: "Sir, We desire to express sincere and grateful thanks to you and all of your command. People living in the area this side of the Channel have followed anxiously the great efforts of the Canadians in the hazardous job of liberating the French Channel Ports. Your success is our relief and we would be particularly pleased if you would kindly pass on our thanks to all ranks. We hope to have an early opportunity of thanking some, if not all, of the boys of your Canadian Forces of the Liberation Army. Good luck and a safe return."

In the evening the bells of the Parish Church rang out with a grandsire double peal for nearly an hour. Chief Inspector Richard Butler wrote in the conclusion of his report: "The month of shelling immediately followed ten weeks of intensive flying bomb attacks, during which Civil Defence Services were operationally engaged on no fewer than 52 occasions, which resulted in the personnel being practically exhausted, and at the minimal operational strength owing to sickness and other wastages.

"Twice during the shelling period it became necessary to retain practically the whole of the personnel on continuous tours of duty, ranging from 18 hours to 48 hours, and in the case of leaders and key personnel on one occasion for 72 hours; it is with a great deal of pride that I am able to say that from the first incident on 1st September to the last shelling incident on 25th September, courage, cheerfulness and efficiency were displayed by all concerned to the highest possible degree.

It would not be proper to draw particular attention to any one service or individual in a report of this nature, as certain recommendations are being dealt with by me separately, but I would, in conclusion, say that the messengers, all under the age of 19; the Rescue Service under the inspiring leadership of Mr T. Creaner; the Casualties Service with their Depot Superintendent Mr R. Hurst; the Transport Service of whole-time and part-time drivers; the wardens and fire guards; the mortuary staff under Mr Cox; Report Centre staff; and the Women's Royal Voluntary Service under Miss B. Butler; have by their example earned the praise and gratitude of the Borough of Folkestone.

"I am, Gentlemen, Your Obedient Servant, Richard Butler
ARP Sub-Controller."

Borough of Folkestone

Official Programme
of the

Victory
Celebrations

8th—14th June, 1946.
PRICE 2d.

EPILOGUE

Their Majesties King George VI and Queen Elizabeth visited Folkestone on Wednesday 18th October 1944, to pay their personal tribute to members of the town's Civil Defence services. There were speeches galore praising the personnel as a whole for their high standard of efficiency throughout the war period and, more especially, the period of intensive cross-Channel shelling which had ended just three weeks before.

The whole town was decorated with bunting and flags, last seen on the accession of George VI to the throne in January 1936. When 80-year-old Mr Pink arrived at his shell-scarred shop in George Lane, he discovered someone had stolen all his bunting during the night. "Please return flags stolen on Oct: 17th" was chalked upon a board outside the ruins of his shop. Mr Pink had added another cryptic message: "Hells Corner — one of the few survivors". No one quite knew what to do with themselves in the couple of months to Christmas. There was an uncanny silence in the town. It seemed too good to be true. There were no explosions and people were actually sleeping in their own bedrooms.

On Friday 22nd December, 550 boys and girls returned to the town from South Wales, after an all day journey from their reception areas. Their return marked the end of the Government's Official Evacuation Scheme for Folkestone's schoolchildren. The public were informed that the whole stretch of Hythe's seafront and beach, from the Lifeboat Station to Seabrook, was now open between sunrise and sunset. Although Folkestone's war had, by and large, finished in September 1944, the Civil Defence Corps remained as a Post War service until disbanded in 1968.

In January 1945, a special constable in the Black Bull Road area was startled to hear the sound of gunfire closeby. Climbing over brick rubble he saw two youths firing a Sten-gun into a stagnant pond on waste ground. Further investigation revealed the youths had stolen 98 rounds of 9 mm ammunition, the Sten-gun, anti-tank shells, grenades and mortar bombs from the Army Drill Hall in Shellons Street. Brought up in an atmosphere of bombs and shells exploding around them, the proximity of troops, airmen and all manner of uniforms, daily observance of aircraft and the fascination of the recognition of them from booklets sold in the newsagents shop on the corner, they saw their own chances of being "in the war" dwindling. They were not criminals, they wanted to be part of the scene they knew so well. As members of the ARP Messenger Unit they had seen at first hand the devastation and chaos left by an exploding shell. They had rubbed shoulders with American gunners clawing away rubble with their bare hands to reach survivors. The eerie scenes of dead bodies lying beneath blankets lit by emergency floodlighting would remain with them for the rest of their lives, as would pictures of beds and tin baths hanging from cracked walls and here and there a picture frame still fixed to the chimneybreast hanging at a crazy angle above a void where once had been the floor. They would remember the Doodlebug damaged by AA fire which dived upon Bridge Street, another which exploded over Princess Street in a ball of orange flame. They would remember the Churchill tank which struck the railings outside the Railway Bell public house, the incendiary bombs falling like a shower of silver fish in the moonlight upon the roofs of houses. When the George Spurgeon School was hit they stepped over the bottles of preserved snakes and lizards which littered the playing field. They had peered out of doorways to watch the dog-fights over the town and dashed out into the streets to pick up the shining brass cannon shell cases. Their prize possessions included bits and pieces of flying bombs which they had man-handled over garden walls and fences while the fragments were still warm to the touch.

And then the exciting weeks before "D-Day", when soldiers charged about in Jeeps and Bren-gun Carriers — when they made their mock attacks upon the already derelict houses, throwing thunder-flashes and grenades with almost complete abandon. At Dover Road, they had removed their caps and had stood to attention whilst an RAF cortège of Union Jack draped coffins slowly passed towards the Junction Station.

They would never forget the large piano that was blown out of the Wonder Tavern, to be thrown with such force as to carry it over the Southern Railway arch to smash onto the Stade. They would remember also the ARP warden attending a boy's head injury in Burrow Road, quite unaware they were standing over an unexploded bomb. And then there were the peculiar antics of one bomb that struck the gable-end of 73 Penfold Road, bounced over 39 Southbourne Road, before finally exploding in Ormonde Road.

Stories of the ARP groups would fill a book in their own right. One concerned "Tiddley-Winks" the cat mascot of the Harbour ARP, who had served with the men and women of that post from the time the first siren sounded. He remained with them throughout the war years. He seemed to know the different warnings and always managed to get to the post before any of the members arrived.

So closes this chronicle by one mind which belatedly, was able to mark the passage of Folkestone's war years, and in the hope that it may contribute something, however small, to aid those who may take up the narrative in greater detail. At least I hope it may constitute a lasting memorial to everyone, man and woman, who served their town in wartime in their inimitable and time-honoured fashion.

ROLL OF HONOUR

A permanent memorial in honour of those civilians killed as a result of enemy action was entrusted, by Royal Charter on February 7th 1941, to the Imperial War Graves Commission.

The Commission relied heavily upon figures submitted by the Registrar-Generals and lists of names were arranged by counties. These lists formed the basis of several volumes and are known as the Roll of Honour.

On 21st February 1956, The Duke of Gloucester, as President of the Imperial War Graves Commission, handed the Roll of Honour to the Dean and Chapter of Westminster. One volume lies open in a Memorial Case where a single page is turned each day.

The Municipal Borough of Folkestone Roll of Honour is, like those of other boroughs, cities and towns, incomplete. The reasons for this are complex but it is a considered judgement that relatives of the deceased have not fully understood the inaccuracies of the official statistics which, in some instances, were never updated.

AIANO, Gladys Lillian, age 47, died 18th November 1940.

ANSELL, Vera Emily Myrtle, age 47, died 17th May 1942.

ARCHARD, Edith, age 56, died 29th May 1941.

ARCHARD, Herbert Benjamin, age 63, died 29th May 1941.

ATKINS, Alfred Benjamin, age 12, died 11th August 1944.

BAILEY, Alice Emma, age 45, died 18th November 1940.

BAILEY, Ellen, age 73, died 18th November 1940.

BAILEY, Frederick, age 61, died 20th March 1941.

BAKER, William, age 17, died 9th November 1942.

BAKER, William Charles, age 32, died 13th November 1940.

BEAL, John, age 81, died 3rd August 1944.

BENTLEY, Diana, age 10, died 6th October 1940.

BISHOP, Hilary, age 49, died 26th August 1940.

BOSS, John Poultney, age 52, died 24th April 1942.

BURVILL, James Robert, age 53, died 3rd July 1944.

BUSH, Alfred Edward, age 57, died 14th September 1944.

BUSHELL, Dorothy Mary, age 16, died 6th October 1940.

COHEN, Gertrude, age 42, died 10th December 1942.

COLEGATE, Alfred, age 68, died 19th November 1940.

COLEGATE, Sophia, age 77, died 18th November 1940.

COOPER, Frederick, age 37, died 23rd September 1942.

CORNISH, Richard, age 66, died 4th January 1940.

CRAUFORF-STUART, Kennedy, Lt.Col., age —, died 21st August 1942.

CRUMP, Daisy, age 49, died 29th May 1941.
COX, Freda Kathleen, age 28, died 6th October 1940.
DICKINSON, William George, age 49, died 15th September 1944.
EARLY, Ronald Leslie, age 20, died 18th November 1940.
EDWARDS, Walter Victor, age 55, died 4th November 1942.
ELLIOTT, Vivienne, age 10 weeks, died 14th September 1944.
FISHER, John, age 53, died 15th August 1942.
FITZGERALD, Edward Desmond, age —, died 27th October 1940.
FITZGERALD, Louisa Marion, age 70, died 27th October 1940.
FOAD, William, age 48, died 4th January 1940.
FOREMAN, Arthur John Earle, age 18, died 11th October 1940.
GARDNER, William John, age 29, died 5th October 1940.
GRIFFIN, Alice, age 29, died 19th March 1941.
GRIFFIN, John Patrick, age 4, died 19th March 1941.
GRIFFIN, Peter William, age 18 months, died 19th March 1941.
GURR, George Albert, age 59, JP, died 29th May 1941.
GURR, Kate Matilda Jane, age 60, died 29th May 1941.
HAMMON, Roger Sidney, age 17, died 21st August 1942.
HART, Edward Richard, age 35, died 5th October 1940.
HART, Louise Marsh, age 17, died 26th August 1940.
HASTINGS, William Charles, age —, died 9th August 1945.
HOLLAWAY, Charles Edwin, age 60, 26th August 1940.
HOLMAN, C.A., age —, died 31st May 1942.
HOPPER, Herbert Charles, age 53, died 9th April 1943.
HOPPER, Millicent, age 53, died 9th April 1943.
HOWLAND, Elsie Elizabeth, age 36, died 8th July 1940.
IBBETT, Vivienne Mary Linsday, age 22, died 15th September 1944.
JONES, Charles John Austen, age 33, died 29th May 1941.
KENDALL, Martha Grace, age 60, died 14th September 1944.
KNIGHT, George Edward, age 79, died 26th August 1940.
KNOTT, Betsy May, age 24, died 29th May 1941.
KNOTT, Colin John, age 18 months, died 29th May 1941.
LAKER, Margaret Carnegie Murrish, age 37, died 5th May 1942.
LAWSON, Alice Emily, age 63, died 3rd July 1944.
LUCKETT, Charles William, age 44, died 18th November 1940.
LUCKETT, Maud Martha, age 47, died 18th November 1940.
MARSH, Florence Elizabeth, age 25, died 29th May 1941.
MASKELL, William, age 71, died 18th November 1940.
MEANEY, Thomas, age 70, died 21st April 1944.
MOCKETT, Daisy Anne, age 47, died 10th September 1944.
MOCKETT, Margaret Susannah, age 80, died 12th September 1944.
MOORE, Albert John, age 49, MM, died 5th October 1940.
MURTON, Esther Hannah, age 63, died 3rd July 1944.

PACKER, Amelia Eleanor, age 52, died 14th September 1944.

PALMER, Frederick Davis, age 65, died 24th May 1944.

PALMER, Mary Ann, age 70, died 24th May 1944.

PEGDEN, Derek John, age 22 months, died 25th September 1943.

PEGDEN, Jeanne Sylvia, age 10, died 25th September 1943.

PEPPER, Thomas, age 57, died 24th September 1942.

PITCHER, Alice, age 61, died 29th May 1941.

PITCHER, Harry, age 64, died 29th May 1941.

POTTEN, Arthur Edward, age 43, died 5th October 1940.

PRINCE, Gerald William, age 17, died 6th October 1940.

PUNYER, Henry Thomas, age 53, died 28th August 1940.

RAINSFORD, Charles Vincent, age 62, died 18th November 1940.

RAINSFORD, Rose Lucie, age 56, died 18th November 1940.

RANSLEY, Cecil Albert, age 37, died 6th November 1941.

RELEN, Albert John, age 61, died 23rd September 1944.

SAUNDERS, George Edward, age 29, died 18th November 1940.

SAYER, Ernest, age 67, died 5th April 1943.

SCOTT, Frederick, age 83, died 5th April 1943.

SIMMS, Charles William, age 30, died 6th October 1944.

SIMPSON, Charlotte Martha, age 66, died 13th September 1944.

SIMPSON, Robert, age 54, died 9th November 1942.

SINSTADT, James William, age 36, died 29th May 1941.

SINSTADT, Winifred Harriett, age 36, died 29th May 1941.

STROUD, William Charles Frederick, age 76, died 5th September 1944.

STUBBINGTON, Charles, age 40, died 18th November 1940.

TAME, Walter Tom, age 86, died 18th November 1940.

TANNER, Vera, age 27, died 6th October 1940.

TAYLOR, Charlotte Eveline, age 71, died 7th January 1941.

TAYLOR, Grace Elizabeth, age 59, died 6th October 1940.

THOMPSON, Harriet May, age 66, died 17th May 1942.

TERRY, A.J., age —, died — July 1940.

TODD, Anne Ethel May, age 19, died 26th August 1940.

UNWIN, William James, age 36, died 5th October 1940.

WARNER, William George, age 40, died 23rd September 1942.

WATKIN-EDWARDS, Rowland, age 63, died 17th May 1942.

WEATHERHEAD, Fred Senr, age 67, died 4th January 1940.

WEATHERHEAD, Fred Jnr, age 41, died 4th January 1940.

WHITE, L.W.P., age —, died — 1942.

WHITE, Sheila Esther, age 9, died 6th September 1940.

WILLIS, Percy, age 61, died 9th April 1943.

WOOD, Mary Harvey, age 84, died 15th August 1944.

CIVIL DEFENCE,

No. 12 (SOUTH EASTERN) REGION.

Office of the Regional Commissioner.

TELEPHONE:
TUNBRIDGE WELLS 3320.

BREDBURY,

MOUNT EPHRAIM,

TUNBRIDGE WELLS.

15th.November,1940.

Dear Mr.Spain,

It is with much pleasure that, at the request of the Minister of Home Security, I inform you that His Majesty the King has been graciously pleased to award you the George Medal in recognition of your gallant conduct in connection with the rescue of a civilian during the air raid on August 26th. 1940.

Mr.Herbert Morrison has asked me to convey to you his personal congratulations on the award of this high honour.

I offer also my own congratulations on the award and I would add that your courage and valuable work on the occasion in question were greatly appreciated.

Yours sincerely,

Deputy Regional
Commissioner.

Police Constable W T.E.Spain.

AWARDS

George Medal
Police Constable William Thomas Elnor SPAIN
Police Constable Cyril A. WILLIAMS
Mr George FENTON (Carpenter)
Dr Robert Lindsay, MA, MB, ChB

British Empire Medal
Chief Inspector Richard J. BUTCHER (ARP Sub-Controller)
Second Officer George FRY (NFS)
Mr Ernest A. WARREN (ARP Warden)
Mr Terence CREANER (Rescue Service Staff Officer)

Order of the British Empire
Mr Norman W. CASTLE (Acting Borough Engineer)

King's Police Medal
Chief Inspector William L. HOLLANDS

Commended in the 'London Gazette' by HM King George VI
Mrs Annie WILLIAMS (ARP Warden)
Mr William DONOVAN (Senior ARP Warden)
Mr Robert W. HOGBEN (ARP Warden)
Mr Albert G. RIGDEN (Engineer, Salter's Laundry)

Establishing humane regulations regarding the treatment of the sick and wounded in war and the status of those who administered it was made in 1864 under the Geneva Convention. Hospitals, ships, vehicles and personnel under military authority were required to display the Geneva Cross — a red cross on a white ground. It was not until 1949 that civilians in war came under the same protection, hence the white ground only seen here on 'Marigold', one of several private cars converted into ambulances and used in Folkestone by the ARP during the last war.

Barbara Cooper, daughter of George Cooper who will be known to Folkestonians as the musician who managed the 'Leas Shelter' orchestra before the Leas Cliff Hall was built, stands beside a 'Sitting Case' car, requisitioned for the First Aid Party.

SUMMARY OF ENEMY ACTION

Air Raid Warnings 2,914
Local Alarm Signals 1,235
Shell Warnings 102
(Shell warning was introduced in Folkestone, 16th November 1942.
Folkestone shelled on 7 occasions prior to that date.)

Air Raids.. 102
HE Bombs 519
Parachute Mines.. 4
Killed... 88
Seriously Injured....................................... 152
Slightly Injured.. 308

Flying Bombs 26   (Destroyed over or on
                                                                           Folkestone)
Flying Bombs 602   (Destroyed seawards of
                                                                           Folkestone)
Killed.. 3
Seriously Injured....................................... 24
Slightly Injured.. 128

Shelling.. 36   (Number of occasions)
Shells on Land 218
Killed.. 32
Serious Injured.. 64
Slightly Injured.. 102

Damage to Property 14,141

Casualty Summary   Killed........................... 123
                              Seriously Injured........ 240
                              Slightly Injured.......... 538
Total 901

This summary of enemy action up to and including 5th October 1944, was
compiled by Lieutenant Colonel C.A. Clark, DSO, MC, Chief Air Raid Warden of
Folkestone.

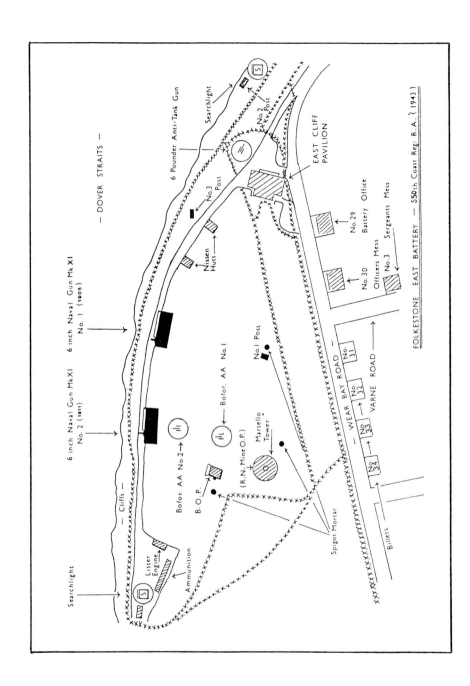

FOLKESTONE EAST BATTERY — 550th Coast Reg. R.A. (1943)

- DOVER STRAITS -

6 inch Naval Gun MkXI
No. 1 (1905)

6 inch Naval Gun MkXI
No. 2 (1911)

6 Pounder Anti-Tank Gun

Searchlight

No. 2 Post

No. 3 Post

Nissen Huts

EAST CLIFF PAVILION

No. 29   Battery Office

No. 30   Officers Mess   No. 3   Sergeants Mess

Bofor. AA No. 1

No. 1 Post

WEAR BAY ROAD

No. 31

No. 32

VARNE ROAD

No. 33

No. 34

Bofor. AA No. 2

B. O. P.

Martello Tower

(R.N. Mine O.P.)

Spigot Mortar

Billets

- Cliffs -

Searchlight

Lister Engine

Ammunition

184

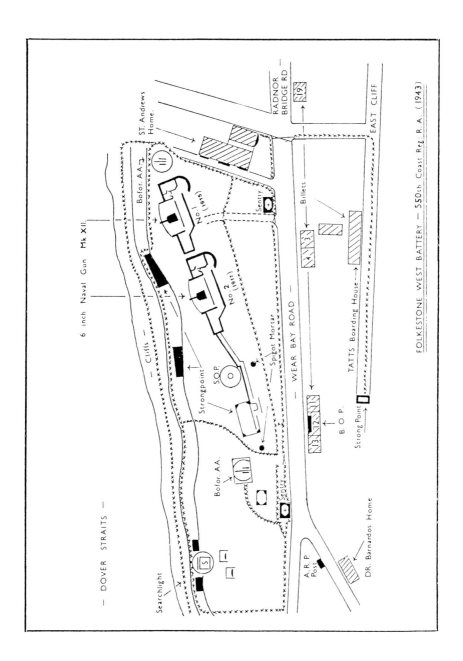

FOLKESTONE WEST BATTERY — 550th Coast Reg. R.A. (1943)

— DOVER STRAITS —

Searchlight

6 inch Naval Gun Mk XII.

Cliffs

Bofor. AA.

St. Andrews Home.

RADNOR BRIDGE RD

No.1 (1915)

No.2 (1917)

Sentry

Billets

EAST CLIFF

Strongpoint

S.O.P.

Spigot Mortar

WEAR BAY ROAD

TATTS Boarding House

Bofor. AA.

B.O.P.

Strong Point

A.R.P. Post

DR. Barnardos Home

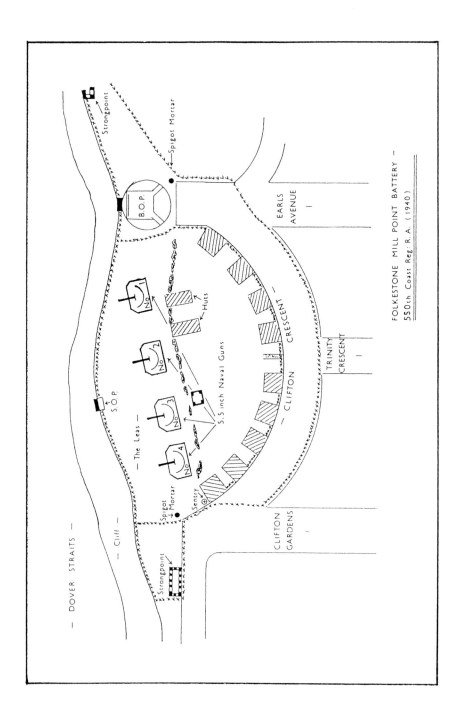

FOLKESTONE MILL POINT BATTERY –
550th Coast Reg: R.A. (1940)

DOVER STRAITS –

– Cliff –

Strongpoint

B.O.P.

Spigot Mortar

– The Leas –

S.O.P.

No.1

No.2

No.3

No.4

Huts

S.5 inch Naval Guns

Spigot Mortar

Sentry

Strongpoint

EARLS AVENUE

TRINITY CRESCENT

– CLIFTON CRESCENT –

CLIFTON GARDENS

186

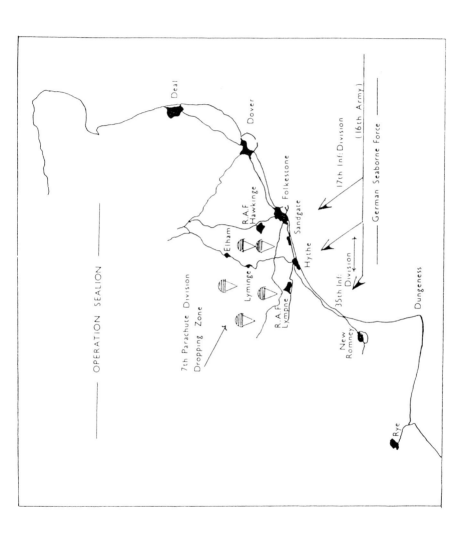

OPERATION SEALION

Deal

Dover

Folkestone

R.A.F Hawkinge

Elham

Sandgate

Hythe

Lyminge

7th Parachute Division Dropping Zone

R.A.F Lympne

35th Inf: Division

New Romney

17th Inf: Division

German Seaborne Force

(16th Army)

Dungeness

Rye

187

GLOSSARY

AA (Ack-ack)	Anti-aircraft guns.
AFS	Auxiliary Fire Service.
ARP	Air Raid Precautions.
BEM	British Empire Medal.
BEF	British Expeditionary Force.
CD	Civil Defence.
CO	Commanding Officer.
DFC	Distinguished Flying Cross.
Flt.Lt.	Flight Lieutenant.
Flg.Off.	Flying Officer.
FW	Focke-Wulf (German fighter).
Gefr.	Gefreiter (Aircraftman 1st class) Luftwaffe.
HAA	Heavy ack-ack.
HE	High Explosive.
HQ	Head Quarters.
IB	Incendiary Bomb.
LDV	Local Defence Volunteers.
NAAFI	Navy, Army, Air Force Institute.
NFS	National Fire Service.
Oberfw.	Oberfeldwebel (Flight Sergeant) Luftwaffe.
PC	Police Constable.
RA	Royal Artillery.
RE	Royal Engineers.
Uffz.	Unteroffizier (Corporal) Luftwaffe.
UXB	Unexploded Bomb.
V1	Flying Bomb.
WVS	Women's Voluntary Service.

BIBLIOGRAPHY

The purpose of this book is to provide a chronology of reference to events which affected the town of Folkestone during the Second World War. To describe events prior to the war years would give an imbalance. Further reference to the bibliography will provide a more detailed selection of books of a specialist nature, and will offer the reader any amount of statistical data.

Divine, David, 'The Nine Days of Dunkirk'; Faber & Faber, London.
'The Folkestone Herald', 'Front Line Folkestone'.
Wilmot, Chester, 'The Struggle for Europe'; Collins, London.
Mason, Francis K., 'Battle over Britain'; McWhirter Twins Ltd, London.
Ramsey, Winston G. (Ed.), 'The Battle of Britain — Then and Now'; Plaistow Press, London.
Ramsey, Winston G. (Ed.), 'The Blitz — Then and Now'; Vol. 1 – 2 – 3; Plaistow Press, London.
Rootes, Andrew, 'Front Line County'; Robert Hale, London.
Newspapers: 'The Folkestone & Hythe District Herald' — Complete issues covering the Second World War.

Meresborough Books

17 Station Road, Rainham, Gillingham, Kent. ME8 7RS
Telephone: Medway (0634) 388812

We are a specialist publisher of books about Kent. Our books are available in most bookshops in the county, including our own at this address. Alternatively you may order direct, adding 10% for post (minimum 30p, orders over £25 post free). ISBN prefix 0 905270 for 3 figure numbers, 094819 for 4 figure numbers. Titles in print December 1990.

HARDBACKS

AIRCRAFT CASUALTIES IN KENT Part One 1939-40 compiled by G.G. Baxter, K.A. Owen and P. Baldock. ISBN 3506. £12.95.

BARGEBUILDING ON THE SWALE by Don Sattin. ISBN 3530. £9.95.

EDWARDIAN CHISLEHURST by Arthur Battle. ISBN 3433. £9.95.

FISHERMEN FROM THE KENTISH SHORE by Derek Coombe. ISBN 3409. £10.95.

THE GILLS by Tony Conway. ISBN 266. £5.95. BARGAIN OFFER £1.95.

JUST OFF THE SWALE by Don Sattin. ISBN 045. £5.95.

KENT CASTLES by John Guy. ISBN 150. £7.50.

KENT'S OWN by Robin J. Brooks. The history of 500 (County of Kent) Squadron of the R.A.A.F. ISBN 541. £5.95.

LIFE AND TIMES OF THE EAST KENT CRITIC by Derrick Molock. ISBN 3077. BARGAIN OFFER £1.95.

THE LONDON, CHATHAM & DOVER RAILWAY by Adrian Gray. ISBN 886. £7.95.

THE NATURAL HISTORY OF ROMNEY MARSH by Dr F.M. Firth, M.A., Ph.D. ISBN 789. £6.95.

A NEW DICTIONARY OF KENT DIALECT by Alan Major. ISBN 274. £7.50.

THE PAST GLORY OF MILTON CREEK by Alan Cordell and Leslie Williams. ISBN 3042. £9.95.

ROCHESTER FROM OLD PHOTOGRAPHS compiled by the City of Rochester Society. Large format. ISBN 975. £7.95.(Also available in paperback ISBN 983. £4.95.)

SHERLOCK HOLMES AND THE KENT RAILWAYS by Kelvin Jones. ISBN 3255. £8.95.

SOUTH EAST BRITAIN: ETERNAL BATTLEGROUND by Gregory Blaxland. A military history. ISBN 444. £5.95. BARGAIN £2.95.

STRATFORD HOUSE SCHOOL 1912-1987 by Susan Pittman. ISBN 3212. £10.00.

TALES OF VICTORIAN HEADCORN or The Oddities of Heddington by Penelope Rivers (Ellen M. Poole). ISBN 3050. £8.95. (Also available in paperback ISBN 3069. £3.95).

TEYNHAM MANOR AND HUNDRED (798-1935) by Elizabeth Selby, MBE. ISBN 630. £5.95.

TROOPSHIP TO CALAIS by Derek Spiers. ISBN 3395. £11.95.

TWO HALVES OF A LIFE by Doctor Kary Pole. ISBN 509. £5.95.

US BARGEMEN by A.S. Bennett. ISBN 207. £6.95.

A VIEW OF CHRIST'S COLLEGE, BLACKHEATH by A.E.O. Crombie, B.A. ISBN 223. £6.95.

STANDARD SIZE PAPERBACKS

BIRDS OF KENT: A Review of their Status and Distribution by the Kent Ornithological Society. ISBN 800. £6.95.
BIRDWATCHING IN KENT by Don Taylor. ISBN 932. £4.50.
THE CANTERBURY MONSTERS by John H. Vaux. ISBN 3468. £2.50.
THE CHATHAM DOCKYARD STORY by Philip MacDougall. ISBN 3301. £6.95.
CHIDDINGSTONE — AN HISTORICAL EXPLORATION by Jill Newton. ISBN 940. £1.95.
A CHRONOLOGY OF ROCHESTER by Brenda Purle. ISBN 851. £1.50.
COBHAM. Published for Cobham Parish Council. ISBN 3123. £1.00.
CRIME AND CRIMINALS IN VICTORIAN KENT by Adrian Gray. ISBN 967. £3.95.
CURIOUS KENT by John Vigar. ISBN 878. £1.95.
CYCLE TOURS OF KENT by John Guy. No. 1: Medway, Gravesend, Sittingbourne and Sheppey. ISBN 517. £1.50.
EXPLORING KENT CHURCHES by John E. Vigar. ISBN 3018. £3.95.
EXPLORING SUSSEX CHURCHES by John E. Vigar. ISBN 3093. £3.95.
FLIGHT IN KENT. ISBN 3085. £1.95.
FROM MOTHS TO MERLINS: The History of West Malling Airfield by Robin J. Brooks. ISBN 3239. £4.95.
THE GHOSTS OF KENT by Peter Underwood. ISBN 86X. (Reprinting)
A HISTORY OF CHATHAM GRAMMAR SCHOOL FOR GIRLS, 1907-1982 by Audrey Perkyns. ISBN 576. £1.95.
KENT AIRFIELDS IN THE BATTLE OF BRITAIN by the Kent Aviation Historical Research Society. ISBN 3247. (Reprinting)
KENT COUNTRY CHURCHES by James Antony Syms. ISBN 3131. £4.50.
KENT COUNTRY CHURCHES CONTINUED by James Antony Syms. ISBN 314X. £5.95.
KENT COUNTRY CHURCHES CONCLUDED by James Antony Syms. ISBN 345X. £5.95.
KENT INNS AND SIGNS by Michael David Mirams. ISBN 3182. £3.95.
LET'S EXPLORE THE RIVER DARENT by Frederick Wood. ISBN 770. £1.95.
LULLINGSTONE PARK: THE EVOLUTION OF A MEDIAEVAL DEER PARK by Susan Pittman. ISBN 703. £3.95.
PENINSULA ROUND (The Hoo Peninsula) by Des Worsdale. ISBN 568. £1.50.
PRELUDE TO WAR: Aviation in Kent 1938-39 by KAHRS. ISBN 3476. £2.50.
RADIO KENT GARDENERS' GUIDE by Harry Smith and Bob Collard. ISBN 3549. £3.95.
REAL ALE PUBS IN KENT by CAMRA in Kent. ISBN 3263. Was £1.95. Now 95p.
SAINT ANDREW'S CHURCH, DEAL by Gregory Holyoake. ISBN 835. 95p.
SHORNE: The History of a Kentish Village by A.F. Allen. ISBN 3204. £4.95.
SIR GARRARD TYRWHITT-DRAKE AND THE COBTREE ESTATE, MAIDSTONE by Elizabeth Melling B.A. ISBN 3344. £1.50.
SITTINGBOURNE & KEMSLEY LIGHT RAILWAY STOCKBOOK AND GUIDE. ISBN 843. 95p.
STEAM IN MY FAMILY by John Newton. ISBN 3417. £4.95.
STOUR VALLEY WALKS from Canterbury to Sandwich by Christopher Donaldson. ISBN 991. £1.95.
TALES OF VICTORIAN HEADCORN — see under hardbacks.
TARGET FOLKESTONE by Roy Humphreys. ISBN 3514. £7.95.
WADHURST: Town of the High Weald by Alan Savidge and Oliver Mason. ISBN 3352. £5.95.
WARTIME KENT 1939-40 compiled by Oonagh Hyndman from the BBC Radio Kent broadcasts. ISBN 3611. £6.95.
WHERE NO FLOWERS GROW by George Glazebrook. ISBN 3379. £2.50.
WHO'S BURIED WHERE IN KENT by Alan Major. ISBN 3484. £5.95.

LARGE FORMAT PICTORIAL PAPERBACKS

ARE YOU BEING SERVED, MADAM? by Molly Proctor. ISBN 3174. £3.50.
AVIATION IN KENT by Robin J. Brooks. ISBN 681. £2.95.
BEFORE AND AFTER THE HURRICANE IN AND AROUND CANTERBURY by Paul Crampton. ISBN 3387. £3.50. BARGAIN £1.95.
THE BLITZ OF CANTERBURY by Paul Crampton. ISBN 3441. £3.50.
EAST KENT FROM THE AIR by John Guy. ISBN 3158. £3.50.
EAST SUSSEX RAILWAYS IN OLD POSTCARDS by Kevin Robertson. ISBN 3220. £3.50.
GEORGE BARGEBRICK Esq. by Richard-Hugh Perks. ISBN 479. £4.50.
HEADCORN: A Pictorial History by the Headcorn Local History Society. ISBN 3271. £3.50.
KENT TOWN CRAFTS by Richard Filmer. ISBN 584. £2.95.
THE LIFE AND ART OF ONE MAN by Dudley Pout. ISBN 525. £2.95.
THE MEDWAY TOWNS FROM THE AIR by Piers Morgan and Diane Nicholls. ISBN 3557. £4.95.
MORE PICTURES OF RAINHAM by Barbara Mackay Miller. ISBN 3298. £3.50.
THE MOTOR BUS SERVICES OF KENT AND EAST SUSSEX — A brief history by Eric Baldock. ISBN 959. £4.95.
OLD BROADSTAIRS by Michael David Mirams. ISBN 3115. £3.50.
OLD CHATHAM: A THIRD PICTURE BOOK by Philip MacDougall. ISBN 3190. £3.50. BARGAIN £1.95.
OLD FAVERSHAM by Arthur Percival. ISBN 3425. £3.50.
OLD GILLINGHAM by Philip MacDougall. ISBN 3328. £3.50.
OLD MAIDSTONE'S PUBLIC HOUSES by Irene Hales. ISBN 533. £2.95. BARGAIN £1.95.
OLD MAIDSTONE Vol.3 by Irene Hales. ISBN 3336. £3.50. BARGAIN £1.95.
OLD MARGATE by Michael David Mirams. ISBN 851. £3.50.
OLD PUBS OF TUNBRIDGE WELLS & DISTRICT by Keith Hetherington and Alun Griffiths. ISBN 300X. £3.50.
PEMBURY IN THE PAST by Mary Standen. ISBN 916. £2.95.
A PICTORIAL STUDY OF ALKHAM PARISH by Susan Lees and Roy Humphreys. ISBN 3034. £2.95.
A PICTORIAL STUDY OF HAWKINGE PARISH by Roy Humphreys. ISBN 328X. £3.50.
A PICTUREBOOK OF OLD NORTHIAM by Lis Rigby. ISBN 3492. £3.95.
A PICTUREBOOK OF OLD RAINHAM by Barbara Mackay Miller. ISBN 606. £3.50.
REMINISCENCES OF OLD CRANBROOK by Joe Woodcock. ISBN 331X. £3.50.
ROCHESTER FROM OLD PHOTOGRAPHS — see under hardbacks.
SMARDEN: A Pictorial History by Jenni Rodger. ISBN 592. £3.50.
THOMAS SIDNEY COOPER OF CANTERBURY by Brian Stewart. ISBN 762. £2.95.
WEST KENT FROM THE AIR by John Guy. ISBN 3166. £3.50.